# FLORIDA IN TURMOIL
# THE TERRIBLE WAR YEARS
# 1861-1865

## BEN H. WILLINGHAM

## Osborn of Jacksonville, LLC

*This book is dedicated to my wife, Erika, who had patience with me during the years of long nights and weekends I spent working on this book instead of helping her.*

# Acknowledgements

None of this would have been possible without the efforts of my editor, Cassy Gray, who worked tirelessly correcting my grammar and word choice.

I wish to also thank the volunteers at the Museum of Southern History who have helped me with research in the museum's library.

My special thanks go to Jeff Sizemore, Editor General of the Military Order of the Stars and Bars, who was a great help to me in getting a lot of the basic information together years ago when I first started this project.

I would be remiss if I didn't recognize all of those loyal supporters of the idea of a book on Florida during those terrible years of war who encouraged me to proceed with the project and see it to its conclusion.

# Table of Contents

# FLORIDA IN TURMOIL
## THE TERRIBLE WAR YEARS
## 1861 – 1865

*A chronicle of the terrible war years in Florida,*
*and the people who came to her defense.*

The Museum of Southern History is an independent, non-profit educational organization. It receives no public funds and is supported only by its membership and the generous donations of those individuals who understand the work of the museum in educating our youth on their history and heritage.

**The Museum of Southern History**
**4304 Herschel Street**
**Jacksonville, FL 32210**
**(904) 388-3574**
**www.museumsouthernhistory.com**

# WHAT IS THE MUSEUM OF SOUTHERN HISTORY?

## MISSION STATEMENT

The Museum of Southern History was established to maintain and perpetuate an educational facility for those who are interested in the history of the United States, its early problems and difficulties in becoming the nation it is today. The museum is dedicated to historical accuracy in presenting the lifestyle and culture of the Antebellum South, a unique civilization, misunderstood by many, belittled and misrepresented by some, but deeply revered by the grateful descendants of the brave men and women whose sacrifices and dedication to a cause that created a chapter in our nation's history that is unmatched.

## WHAT DOES THE MUSEUM DO?

The Museum of Southern History attempts to fill in the enormous gap in current education as relates to the War Between the States era. Schools spend little time on this subject, which is the backbone of our Nation today. Special attention is given to the education of young people as groups of school children are given basic education in our nation's history in the hope that they will better understand and perhaps develop an interest in learning more about their history.

After the presentation, the children are given an opportunity to handle and fire the old muskets in the courtyard behind the Museum. Annually, approximately 3,000 young school students participate in the educational programs. Many individual visitors come to the museum, where we have the opportunity to fill them in on what they missed during their education.

More information is available: www.museumsouthernhistory.com

# PART I

## The Road to Secession
## and
## Life in a New Country

# 1

## FLORIDA ON THE EVE OF WAR

When the United States of America was established in 1789, the thirteen states were the creators of the Federal government. But by 1860, the Federal government was the creator of the large majority of the States. In 1789, the Federal government derived all the powers delegated to it by the Constitution from the States. In 1860, a majority of the states derived all their powers and attributes as states from Congress under the Constitution.

Power was the object, even back then. States were admitted to increase the power of regions and politicians. By 1860, the controlling power in the Federal government had been transferred from the South to the industrialized North, and the taxation policies enacted by Congress penalized the South to the advantage of the North.

The emotion-packed events of the 1850s foreshadowed the tragic years that were soon to engulf the nation. The great Whig party, which had so strongly upheld the national idea, disintegrated and the Republican Party, which rose to take its place, accepted a platform which inflamed an already agitated South.

The Kansas-Nebraska controversy, the Dred Scott Decision, the Lincoln-Douglas debates were coals added to fires already blazing under cauldrons of suspicion and distrust.

Then on October 16, 1859, John Brown, a man who many thought was a victim of mental delusions, and his followers seized the United States arsenal at Harper's Ferry. Although this plan to free the slaves was doomed from the start, the news of the raid caused a wave of fear and revulsion to spread throughout the South. Secessionists used the raid to win over many conservatives who were still reluctant to support any action that might destroy the Union.

Here was concrete evidence that abolitionists intended to set the slaves upon their masters and to forcibly overthrow the institution which was at the base of society.

The tensions between North and South had become so great that the admirable art of compromise, which had hitherto preserved the American experiment of democratic government, was failing to function. Only disaster could result. No part of the country was isolated from the slavery and state rights controversies which were raging.

1860 was a year of crisis. In the South, states were rapidly severing the invisible bonds which had held the Union together for seventy-seven years. The people of Florida, although they were living in the newest of the slave-holding territories, were caught up in this maelstrom and became a part of the surging tide that carried the country into the War Between the States.

# 2
## THE CORWIN AMENDMENT

The recent discovery of a letter from newly inaugurated President Abraham Lincoln to the Governor of Florida has generated renewed interest in Lincoln's views toward slavery. The letter, found at the Lehigh County Historical Society in Allentown, Pennsylvania, is from Lincoln to Governor Madison Stark Perry. Accompanying the letter was an authenticated copy of a Joint Resolution to amend the Constitutionof the United States. What was this amendment, and what was Lincoln's role in its attempted ratification?

On December 4, 1860, President James Buchanan requested Congress to create a special Committee of Thirty-Three with each state seating a member on the committee. The purpose of the committee was to craft a compromise to prevent the secession of Southern slave states from the Union. Congressman Charles Francis Adams of Massachusetts introduced a version of a constitutional amendment first (unsuccessfully) proposed by Senator Henry Seward of New York. This amendment, as written, would prohibit future constitutional amendments from interfering with slavery where it already existed (i.e. in the South).

The proposal was favorably voted by the Committee of Thirty-Three and was reported to the full House on January 21, 1861, by committee chairman Thomas Corwin, an Ohio Republican. In the Senate, Seward took the lead in sponsoring the amendment.

In a meeting with Thurlow Weed, a masterful political organizer, publisher of the *Evening Journal*, and the man who controlled the Whig Party and Seward's Republican ally in New York, Lincoln offered three compromise proposals, and Weed passed this information to Seward. Upon his return to the Senate, Seward introduced Lincoln's compromises to the Senate committee. One of the resolutions was that no amendment shall be made to the Constitution which would authorize or give Congress the power to abolish or interfere with a state's domestic institutions, including that of persons held to labor or service by the laws of said state. In other words, the amendment would forever guarantee the right of the Southern people to own slaves.

With much debate, the Corwin Amendment, as it was known, was passed both houses of Congress, the House on February 21, 1861, by a vote of 133 to 65, and the Senate on March 2, 1861, by a vote of 24 to 12, two days before Lincoln took office.

The Corwin Amendment was one of three attempts to resolve the secession crisis between Lincoln's election in November 1860 and the commencement of hostilities in April 1861. Buchanan signed the Amendment on March 3, 1861, his last day in office. (The Constitution does not require presidential approval for proposed amendments).

In his inaugural address, Lincoln noted Congressional approval of the Corwin Amendment and stated that he had no objection to its being made express and irrevocable. This statement was not a departure from Lincoln's views on slavery. He did not believe that, as president, had the power to eliminate slavery where it already existed. By implicitly supporting the Corwin Amendment, Lincoln hoped to convince the South that he would not move to abolish slavery and, at a minimum, keep the Border States of Maryland, Virginia, Tennessee, Kentucky, and North Carolina from seceding.

Lincoln's March 16 letters to the governors did not oppose the proposed Thirteenth Amendment (the Corwin Amendment served as the Thirteenth Amendment's second draft). After Lincoln was inaugurated, he sent a copy of the joint resolution to amend the Constitution to the governors and requested they take the necessary action to have the amendment ratified. If anything, this is confirmation that Lincoln failed to recognize the real reasons behind secession. Yes, slavery was an issue, and if it were the only issue, the ratification of the Corwin Amendment would have taken care of the differences. The primary issues were taxes, tariffs, and the states' rights to govern themselves. But Lincoln needed the revenue collected from the South to run the Federal government.

After the firing on Fort Sumter and Lincoln's call for troops, Virginia and Tennessee, among others, seceded. The war began and the purpose of the Corwin Amendment was greatly reduced. However, Ohio and Maryland ratified the Corwin Amendment, and the 1862 Illinois Constitutional Convention endorsed it. As the draft did not contain the usual termination date for non-action, it still remains as an open matter before Congress. It is obviously not realistic that the Corwin Amendment would be activated and sent for ratification. Still, it is an interesting part of history.

This snapshot of March 1861 shows Lincoln's last attempt to restore the Union while maintaining his party's platform of seventeen principles, ten of which related to the Free Soil Principles, a political party dedicated to free soil, free men, and not allowing any new states to become slave holding states, slavery, the Fugitive Slave Act, and the preservation of the Union. The Freesoilers emphasized the threat slavery posed to free white labor and northern businessmen in the new western territories. The Free Soil Party was not inconsequential electing two Senators and fourteen Representatives to the thirty-first Congress before it was absolved into the Republican Party.

The remainder of the platform related to protective tariffs, the Homestead Act, freedom of immigration into the United States, internal improvements in infrastructure, and the construction of the Pacific railroad. Most of these expenditures would be made in the Northern and Western states with money paid by the Southern states.

As there were almost no representatives from the Southern states present at the Republican Party Convention where the platform was conceived, it is understandable that Southern interests were not represented in the adopted platform. While personally indifferent on the subject of slavery, Lincoln believed the Constitution supported it. His support of the Corwin Amendment attempted to codify that belief, but the War Between the States changed his opinion on presidential power. As war became a reality, Lincoln seems to have forgotten the existence of the Constitution as he assumed powers not envisioned by our founding fathers.

On January 1, 1863, Lincoln issued the Emancipation Proclamation, which did not free any slaves, as it referred only to the states in rebellion, over which he had no authority, and did not free the slaves in any of the states that had not seceded. In 1865, Lincoln supported the third draft of the Thirteenth Amendment, which declared slavery illegal. This draft was not passed until after Lincoln's death.

# 3
## FLORIDA SECEDES FROM THE UNION

The U.S. Constitution and the Bill of Rights, largely the product of Southern minds, did not forbid secession. If it had, the Constitution would probably have never been ratified. The authors of these documents wanted to preserve the rights of the individual states as sovereign entities and their people being able to govern themselves in a Democratic system.

The question of secession had long been an issue in the Union. It was definitely not a regional issue. Various New England states had threatened to leave the Union. The first time was in 1814 and the last in 1857 over an import tariff dispute.

Prior to the 1860 election, throughout Florida, public meetings were held to discuss what should be done in the event the Democratic candidate lost the election. The clear sentiment was for secession. When the news arrived that the Republican ticket had won, public meetings were again held all over the state. The discussion was not should Florida succeed but how quickly could it be legally done.

On November 8, at a public meeting, the citizens of Fernandina declared that Lincoln's election was the first step in the dissolution of the Union, and a similar meeting in Jefferson County favored secession if necessary to protect Southern rights.

At town meetings in St. Augustine (November 17) and Ocala (November 26), citizens added their resolutions to the General Assembly to provide for a Convention of Delegates to consider the expediency of dissolving Florida's connection with the Union. The Whigs joined the Democrats in denouncing the selection of Lincoln, while Democratic newspapers almost unanimously demanded state action against that party of fanatics who had deliberately threatened to force Florida into an admission of the equality, socially, and politically, of the slave.

Opposition to immediate secession was publicly expressed by a few prominent Floridians. Richard Keith Call, staunch Whig and strong Union Nationalist, wrote many letters to Middle Florida newspapers urging resistance against Northern oppression by armed revolution within the existing government rather than by secession. Federal Judge William Marvin of Key West opposed the idea of secession and exercised influence in fostering union sentiment in the Keys. David Shelby Walker, an associate justice of the Florida Supreme Court, was opposed to the idea and privately exercised his opinion to others, though his opposition was not as violent as Call.

But the sentiment for secession overwhelmed the small voices of the Unionists, particularly when Governor Madison Perry, Governor-elect John Milton, and Congressman-elect R.B. Hilton were on record by the middle of November for immediate separation. With the Federal government in control of the Republican Party, Southerners believed that Federal control of slavery in the territories was but a minor goal of the abolitionists, who meant to finally destroy slavery in the Southern states.

On November 26, the General Assembly convened in regular session at Tallahassee. Governor Perry devoted his entire message to the necessity for secession at once, as an indecisive wait for an aggressive act by the Federal government might well invite the disaster which the slaves of Santo Domingo had inflicted upon the white inhabitants of that island. Perry asked the legislature to enact legislation for the election of delegates to a constituent assembly which, in turn, might take proper action toward protecting the rights of the people of Florida. Perry also recommended reorganization of the state militia and the appropriation of $100,000 as a military fund for the ensuing year. The legislature quickly acquiesced to the requests of the Chief Executive by passing laws calling for the election of delegates to a convention to be convened on January 3,

1861, the reorganization of the militia, and for the appropriation of $100,000 for the munitions of war.

Perry issued a proclamation on November 30 providing for the election of delegates on December 22. The Governor then left for South Carolina to arrange for the purchase of guns and ammunition and to meet with Southern leaders who had assembled in Charleston to observe the secession convention in the Palmetto State.

In the short campaign for the selection of delegates, the predominant issue was whether secession should be immediate by Florida alone or delayed until Georgia, Alabama, and other Southern states had taken action on the movement.

Wilkinson Call, nephew of R.K. Call, and four others ran on a People's Ticket in Leon County. They pledged to submit the action of the convention to a popular vote. Young Call made a number of speeches on behalf of popular approval of the work of the forthcoming convention, but to no avail. The popular appeal of the secession movement was reflected in the November masthead of the St. Augustine *Examiner*, which read: "The Secession of the State of Florida," "The Dissolution of the Union," and "The Formation of a Southern Confederacy."

The sentiments of the Florida Congressional delegation in Washington appeared to have followed those of their constituents in calling for a state referendum on the issue of secession rather than to have led Floridians in the matter of immediate secession.

Senator David Yulee, considered a radical, wrote:

> *If the modern Republicans succeed in acquiring possession of the Federal government, it will be the duty of the Southern states to secede... until new guaranties of their rights can be obtained; and in failure of this to seek their safety in a new Union of sympathizing and homogeneous States.*

Yulee belonged to the large minority of southern leaders who, in 1860-1861, believed that separation from the old Union and formation of a new Southern Union could be accomplished peacefully.

The Tallahassee *Sentinel* reported in October 1860 that Yulee had stated to the Florida Senate that if there is no peace in the land or any general harmony between the states, Florida should arrange at once for living in peace or parting in peace. However, a month later, Yulee wrote a letter to the General Assembly, then about to convene, of his intention to promptly and joyously return home to assist the state on secession.

Senator Stephen Russell Mallory had remained somewhat aloof of the turmoil. On several occasions, the senior Senator spoke on the floor of the Senate in support of the Southern rights issue, but never with the earlier radical enthusiasm of Yulee. In 1858, Mallory stated that Republican control which infringed on Southern rights would encourage every effort on his part to induce secession of the affected states. He later wrote that he had believed in secession as a right resulting from state sovereignty, but that he regarded secession as only another name for revolution.

Representative George S. Hawkins, however, became a fire-eating radical and pumped for immediate secession. He refused to serve on a joint committee created to compromise on the differences between the sections. He proudly stated that the call for a state convention in Florida was ample proof that a sovereign state could well settle such important questions at home. Hawkins, unlike Yulee and Mallory, signed the address of thirty Southern congressmen, which advised their electors to secede and establish a Southern nation because the triumph of the Republican party forebode the future strangulation of Southern rights with a denial of equality under the Constitution and the laws of Congress.

In the short campaign for the election of convention delegates, opposition to secession was negligible. If there was an issue, the public discussion revolved around the proposition of immediate secession. The Perry administration, press, and pulpit urged rapid action.

When the South Carolina convention voted for secession on December, many Floridians were convinced that the gauntlet had been laid down. Alabama, Mississippi, and Georgia had also called conventions, and Louisiana and Virginia had called special sessions of their legislatures. As a result of the special election, the delegates were divided, with a third of convention membership in the moderate group and several delegates who wavered between cooperation and immediate secession.

The convention met to organize on January 3, 1861. Tallahassee was flooded with visitors from all over the state, as well as Commissioners E.C. Bullock of Alabama and L.W. Spratt of South Carolina. Edmund Ruffin, a rabid fire-eater from Virginia, attended as an unofficial observer and recorded a day-to-day account of the proceedings in his diary.

Sixty of the sixty-nine delegates were present on the first day when a temporary organization was made. There was no meeting on January 4 in deference to President Buchanan's request that the day be observed in fasting and humiliation. Ruffin wrote:

> On account of the political dangers and disasters now impending and to be produced not by Northern abolitionists, but by the spirit of resistance and disunion of the Southern states. The very appointment of the day and service is a rebuke and censure of the seceding states.

It would appear that the convention delegates and state officials used the day of fast and humiliation to confer on the action necessary to seize the various Federal military installations in the state. Federal forces at Pensacola were sufficient enough to keep Pensacola in Union hands. The strength of the Union forces and Union sentiment at Key West secured the town for the Federals throughout the war. The political situation made unwise any other military action as that would have been seen as an act of war, not something the South desired.

In Washington, Yulee and Mallory wrote the War Department for information on the strength of the Federal fortifications and garrisons in Florida, but such intelligence was denied them on the basis of classified matter of interest to the armed forces.

On January 5, Yulee wrote to Joseph Finegan, a business associate and a delegate to the convention, regarding the occupation of the forts and arsenals within the state and especially naval stations and forts at Pensacola. Yulee urged Finegan (who later became a Confederate general) to seek the aid of Georgia troops in the seizure of the forts and the arsenal at Chattahoochee. Yulee also urged the establishment of a confederation of Southern States and the formation of a Southern army for the defense of the South.

Shortly after this, and even before the passage of the secession ordinance, the arsenal at Chattahoochee and Fort Marion at St. Augustine were seized by state troops.

When the secession convention resumed its work on January 5, Judge John C. McGehee of Madison County received forty-seven of the fifty-seven votes cast for president and took the chair. McGehee, an ardent Southern rights spokesman, delivered a stirring address in which the threats to slavery arguments of the Southern states were reiterated once again. He found slavery to be the element of all value, a value whose destruction obliterated property. But the peculiar institution meant value to only 5,000 slave holders. The non-slaveholders feared the abolition of slavery as the end of the control of the Negro; they feared the consequences of the social equality of abolition and likened such an eventuality to the horrors of the Santo Domingo and other insular slave insurrections.

After McGehee's speech, the convention was organized with nine standing committees and several lesser officials. McQueen

McIntosh of Apalachicola, who had resigned a federal judgeship on the Republican victory in November, introduced a resolution upholding the right of secession and the necessity of Florida's exercising the right in view of the national political crisis. Two days later, the resolution was adopted, and the chair appointed a committee to prepare an ordinance of secession.

The secession ordinance reached the convention floor on January 9. Jackson Morton and George T. Ward, former Whigs, led a fight of the more conservative members to delay action until Georgia and Alabama had seceded and to require a popular referendum of the electors of the state on the measure. Both proposals were defeated: the delay, thirty-nine to thirty and the referendum, forty-one to twenty-six.

The debate was heated at times, but clearly the sympathy lay with the secessionists who felt Florida should lead rather than follow her neighboring states. The cooperationists, seeing that immediate action could not be blocked, declared their intention to vote for the secession ordinance because they believed there needed to be political unanimity on such a weighty issue. On January 10, the ordinance was passed by a vote of sixty-two to seven.

A committee was convened to write the actual language of the ordinance, which was also passed on January 10. The language was simple and proclaimed that Florida had withdrawn from the United States of America and is henceforth an independent nation.

Before adjourning, the convention, by resolution, appointed the judges of the Florida Supreme Court to direct the enrolling of the ordinance. The judges, in turn, directed that the ordinance be enrolled on parchment and requested Miss Elizabeth M. Eppes, a lineal descendant of the immortal author of the first Declaration of Independence, to bind the document with blue ribbon.

On the following day, sixty-four members of the convention proceeded to the east portico of the Capitol where the ceremony of signing the ordinance of secession was completed. The ceremony took place before Governor-Elect Milton, the members of the legislature, Supreme Court, the governor's cabinet, and many citizens. After the last member had signed, the state seal was affixed, and McGehee announced that Florida was a free, sovereign, and independent state and that all connections with the United States were at an end.

Secession was the occasion for spontaneous celebrations in Tallahassee and other towns throughout the state. Parades, gun salutes, numerous toasts, and speeches were in evidence as the jubilation over secession spread.

The news of Florida's secession reached Washington by telegraph, and Yulee and Mallory refrained from participation in the proceedings of the Senate, but did not make a formal withdrawal until January 21. In his farewell speech, Yulee reminded the Senate that one of the conditions of the cession of Florida from Spain to the United States was that the residents of the territory should be admitted into the Union on terms of equality with the citizens of that nation. Thus, in seceding, Florida was but exercising the equality gained on entrance into the Union in 1845.

Mallory was more eloquent in his farewell:

> *From the Union, governed by the Constitution as our fathers made it, there breathes not a secessionist upon her soil, but a deep sense of injustice, inequality, and insecurity... is brought home to the reason and patriotism of her people; and to secure and maintain these rights which the Constitution no longer accords them, they have placed the State of Florida out of the Confederacy... We seek not to war upon or to conquer you; and we know that you cannot conquer us.*

Before the convention adjourned, Perry was authorized to appoint four counselors of state. He selected McGehee, Jackson Morton, John Beard, and Finegan. As the convention could not agree on delegates to the convention of the seceded states to be held at Montgomery, Perry appointed Jackson Morton, Patton Anderson, and James B. Owens.

The congressional delegation of Mallory, Yulee, and Hawkins was made a commission to negotiate with Federal officials for the transfer of the United States military and naval installations to the Nation of Florida.

On February 4, the delegates from the seceding states met at Montgomery, Alabama, and later agreed upon a Provisional Government for the Confederate States of America, with a Constitution , which was reported to the states. Jefferson Davis was chosen president and Alexander H. Stevens vice president, both being inaugurated on February 18.

The Florida convention reassembled on January 26 and, on January 28, unanimously adopted the Confederate Constitution; thus, Florida became a member of the Provisional Government. On March 11, 1861, the Confederate Congress adopted the Constitution and reported it to the Florida convention.

On April 18, the convention met again at Tallahassee and, in four days, had again ratified the Confederate Constitution unanimously. From the minutes of the convention, one can see the actual business that was conducted. The state was divided into two congressional districts, and policies were established regulating public lands, fortifications, railroads, and education. Modifications to the state constitution were prepared so they could be presented to the people of the state for ratification.

On April 12, the first gun of the War Between the States was fired at Fort Sumter in Charleston Harbor. Three days later, Lincoln called for 75,000 militiamen to put down the rebellion in the Southern states.

In Florida, the Perry administration carried on until October, while the three Florida members in the Provisional Confederate Congress served until February 17, 1862. When Anderson and

George T. Ward resigned. Ward returned to Richmond and resumed his seat, while John P. Sanderson took Patton's seat. James B. Owens and Jackson Morton served out their one-year terms.

Augustus E. Maxwell and James M. Baker served as senators through the four sessions of the First Congress and the two sessions of the Second Congress, all of which were held at Richmond. Robert B. Hilton served as a representative in both Congresses while James B. Dawkins and John M. Martin divided the term of the second representative in the First Congress and S. St. George Rogers was Hilton's colleague in the Second Congress.

The *Florida Civil War Centennial Commission* established by Governor Farris Bryan in 1960 attempted to clarify the political leanings of each of Florida's leadership during the war. Initially Jackson Morton and George T. Ward had been Whigs but became Constitutional Unionists. James B. Owens, John P. Sanderson, and John M. Martin were Democrats. Following their terms in Congress, Patton Anderson, Jackson Morton, George T. Ward, and John M. Martin served honorably in the Confederate Army.

Certainly none of the states of the Confederacy approached its destiny with higher expectations or more undaunted courage than Florida. Once having pledged her allegiance to the Confederate States of America, there was no turning back.

# 4
## THE SOUTH'S BEST KEPT SECRET

U nder our Federalism system, each state was given two senators, but the number of congressmen was determined by direct election, with the number of congressmen based on the state's population. Northern congressmen wanted to bring Iowa and its large population into the Union, but to do so, a new Southern state had to be admitted to maintain the agreed upon balance of slave and non-slave states as dictated by the 1820 Missouri Compromise.

Florida's population was 57,951, well under the required population total required to join the Union. So, an exception was made to allow Florida into the Union. With Florida came Iowa, further shifting power away from the Southern states. Less than three months after Florida joined the Union, her first elected Governor William D. Mosely (from Jefferson County) spoke of the storm clouds over the horizon. He warned the people of Florida should never give up their rights to govern themselves as a sovereign state. Mosely knew where Florida was headed.

In 1859, the legislature declared that Florida would support the other Southern States in their on-going struggle for states' rights. The Morrill Tariff was passed and signed into law by President James Buchanan on March 2, 1861, but it had been a key issue for the new Republican Party and hotly debated during the 1860 election. It was strongly favored by the industrialists and factory workers as it would limit competition from low cost areas. It was violently opposed by Southerners, especially the cotton planters. In effect, the Morrill Tariff raised rates to protect and encourage Northern industry but increased the tariff on Southern goods from eighteen to forty percent. This new tariff replaced the 1857 tariff, which had been written to benefit the South. The Morrill Tariff remained in effect until the adoption of the Revenue Act of 1913.

Florida and other Southern states sold cotton in the world markets at competitive prices but were forced to buy their shoes, clothing, and other necessities in the import tariff-protected markets of the North. The Northern tariff industrialists wanted to buy in an open market and sell in a closed one. The Southern cotton planters wanted to buy and sell in a free market. Furthermore, the Northern industrialists wanted governmental help in protecting its market from imported goods from Europe.

By 1860, cotton was the basis of Florida's economy. Closely allied with this was the development of the naval stores industry and lumbering. Florida exported cotton, corn, cattle, leather, horses, turpentine, and pitch and imported almost everything she used except vegetables, corn meal, and forage. Her ports were Jacksonville and Fernandina on the Atlantic and St. Marks, Apalachicola, and Pensacola on the Gulf from which goods were shipped to the North and West; as well as directly to Europe and the British Isles.

At the same time, the population had grown to 140,427, which broke down to about 65,000 slaves and 80,000 whites. Only three communities had a population of 2,000 or greater. Railroads had been built prior to the war from Tallahassee to St. Marks, from Jacksonville to Pensacola, and from Fernandina to Cedar Keys.

In proportion to her white population, Florida contributed very generously to the armies of the Confederacy: eleven regiments of infantry (900-1200 men); seven batteries of artillery (four guns each); three regiments of cavalry; approximate total of 15,000 men; more than 110% of her military aged population. Battalions were sent to the Army of Northern Virginia; Departments of South Carolina, Georgia and Florida; and the Army of Tennessee, and, although no battalions were sent to the Army of Trans-Mississippi, their commanding general was a Floridian, Edmund Kirby Smith. Tiny Florida, as she was known back then, acquitted herself very well.

As an example, on the third day at Gettysburg, the Florida 2nd, 5th, and 8th were sandwiched between General Ambrose Ransom Wright's Georgians on their left and General Cadmus Wilcox's Alabamians on their right as they advanced on Cemetery Ridge. It's still debated as to whether the Georgians or the Floridians reached the highest point that day, but what is not debated is the fact that Florida experienced the highest percentage of casualties of any unit at Gettysburg.

Florida was the only state not to hold back troops for its own defense. Governor Milton felt it best to support the war in the North rather than defend Florida's coastline. There were only a few small groups of local cavalry along with old men and young boys left to defend the entire state.

There were 182 engagements fought on Florida soil. With the exception of the first battle at Pensacola, the Confederates prevailed in all of the rest of the engagements in spite of very limited manpower.

★ ★ ★

The overextended Confederate government found it too difficult to adequately defend the thinly populated southernmost state with its vast coastline. By the end of 1863, the Federals had taken control of the area east of the St. Johns River.

The city of Jacksonville was not defended by the Confederates, and the Federals captured the city on their time table, but they were continually under attack by Confederates any time they ventured out of the protection of the city and Union gunboats.

Confederate cavalry attacks caused the Federals to abandon Jacksonville only to return again as the St. Johns River was the gateway into the southern areas of the state. This too was problematic as the Confederate cavalry was successful in sinking a number of Federal ships as they attempted to navigate up river.

The Federals seemed to believe that if they went up the St. Johns River, the slaves would flock to their colors in their desire to go north to join the fight against the Confederates. On one such expedition, not finding any black volunteers to go with them, the Federals herded what slaves they did find and placed them in a stockade between Palatka and Jacksonville. Florida's legendary Captain J.J. Dickison arrived during the night with his small band of cavalry and, after a brief skirmish with the Federals, freed the slaves who happily and voluntarily returned to their plantations and homes.

The state held importance to both sides. For the Confederates, Florida became a critical source of food. By 1863, cattle drives guarded by the cow cavalry funneled 155,000 head of cattle northward toward Confederate commissaries. Citrus and sweet potatoes helped soldiers stave off the ravages of scurvy. Salt extracted from seawater was required for food preservation.

For the North, Florida offered a political opportunity. Toward the end of 1863, Lincoln's reelection was not all that certain. Lincoln believed that if Federal forces could invade Florida, the Unionists within her borders that would enthusiastically cause Florida to rejoin the Union, bolster his reelection, and strike a devastating blow to the struggling Confederacy.

Federal efforts to reach Tallahassee were in vain as the Federal Army would experience a major defeat at Olustee on their way from Jacksonville to Tallahassee. Other efforts from St. Marks on the Gulf of Mexico would be repelled by students at the Battle of Natural Bridge. Lincoln was reelected in spite of the Federal failure to capture Florida and Tallahassee. The interior of the state remained in southern hands until the war was over.

At the end of the war, Tallahassee was the last Southern capital east of the Mississippi to surrender to the Federals, and the only one not to be captured by the Federals during the war.

# 5
## THE OUTBREAK OF WAR

Even as the secession convention sat, the civil and military leaders of the various sections of the state were preparing for action. Governor Perry had ordered the seizure of the Federal arsenal at Chattahoochee, Fort Marion at St. Augustine, and Fort Clinch at Fernandina. State control of all three was accomplished by January 8, 1861. The seizure of these posts was relatively simple since none were garrisoned with more than a handful of soldiers. At Pensacola and Key West, however, the Federal forces had begun preparations for defense against seizure even before the convention assembled. The presence of the navy yard and the three forts on the best protected and deepest harbor of the Gulf Coast made control of Pensacola and fortifications a prize of high value.

When news of the secession ordinance reached Key West, the fifty troops on the island were moved inside Fort Taylor. Although turbulent and aggressive feelings existed among the Southern sympathizers, no determined act to expel the forces was ever made.

Without orders, the commanding officer at Fort Barrancas abandoned the mainland fortifications and transferred his command of one hundred men to Fort Pickens on Santa Rosa Island. From the island, the Federal forces could guard the entrance to Pensacola Bay.

On the tiny islands of Tortugas, almost seventy miles west of Key West, the War Department had conceived an American Gibraltar. Fort Jefferson on Garden Key had been under construction for fifteen years before Florida seceded. The fort was a mighty six-sided high fort – a super-fortification of 250 guns to be manned with a war complement of 1,500 men. By the eve of the war, the Federal government had spent $1,250,000 on the fort.

When the secession ordinance was signed, only thirty men on Tortugas remained loyal to the United States. On January 19, a transport brought artillerymen and guns from Boston to strengthen the fort's defenses. Though repeatedly challenged by Confederate privateers during the war, Fort Jefferson remained in Federal hands and helped to cut the Confederate lifeline between the Atlantic seaboard and the Mississippi River and Gulf ports. Later, Fort Jefferson became Devil's Island and the home of a number of celebrated prisoners.

★ ★ ★

Through the winter of 1860-61, both before and after Florida had seceded, military companies were organized in all of the state's towns and counties. After secession, the troops were mustered into the Army of Florida (state militia) and held ready for future call. Companies of Minute Men were formed throughout the state and were:

> ...accepted by Perry as part of the state militia even though they operated more on the principle of a home guard. All companies at this time were created and equipped by private funds which the governor promised to repay from state funds upon their acceptance into the militia. Governor Perry issued many commissions to his friends throughout the state; and upon his recommendation, the state legislature passed a bill on February 14, 1861, which allowed lieutenants and captains holding commissions to enlist volunteers in their districts.

Both the governments of the seceded states and the Confederacy held the belief that the conflict between North and South would be of short duration. Volunteers enlisted for a term of twelve months. When the Confederate States Army was created in March 1861, the president was empowered to call on the militia of the states to repel invasion and enlist 100,000 volunteers as national troops for a term of one year.

Florida and Confederate forces occupied the evacuated forts of Barrancas and McRee, and, on January 12, demanded and received the surrender of the Pensacola Navy Yard. The Federal troops at Fort Pickens, however, refused to surrender, and Florida and Confederate forces hesitated to attack the fortification for fear of bloodshed and subsequent charges of opening the hostilities. Telegrams from Yulee and Mallory advised a movement on Fort Pickens at the time of Florida's secession, but later, they reversed their stand and advised that nothing radical should be done in order to forestall incidents leading to war before the Confederacy was ready.

Until Buchanan left office, a Fort Pickens truce was observed under which neither side agreed to reinforce or attack the fort on Santa Rosa Island. When Lincoln became president, he decided to disregard, under cover, the Buchanan promises. On April 12, reinforcements were moved into Fort Pickens by small boats from ships standing in the Gulf of Mexico. Four days later, 1,000 men entered Fort Pickens, while the crews of four Union warships, standing off the bar, raised the total Federal forces to 2,000. Any chance for the Confederates to seize Pickens had passed.

On March 7, General Braxton Bragg was given command of the Provisional Army of the Confederate States on Pensacola Bay. National troops were raised by requisition. State governors were encouraged to organize military units in their own bailiwicks to be transferred into the Confederate army.

The first requisitions for Confederate troops were made on March 9. The requisition was for 5,000 men for duty at Pensacola. Under this requisition, Florida's first quota was for 500 men. The 1st Florida Infantry was mustered into the Confederate army on April 5. By July 1, the Confederate government had requisitioned an additional 5,000 Florida troops.

The first Florida offense of the war occurred on the night of September 2. A raiding party from Fort Pickens boarded the navy yard dry dock and burned a repair vessel. Less than two weeks later, three launches loaded with sailors from the USS *Colorado* reached the Confederate schooner *Judah* moored at the navy yard docks. After fierce fighting, the Federals burned the ship. Three of the raiders were killed and twelve wounded – the first war casualties in Florida.

On October 9, Bragg ordered a thousand man raid on the Federal encampment in the rear of Fort Pickens. The Confederates surprised the Federals, but the ensuing fight ended in a draw. Both sides suffered relatively high casualties.

On November 22, artillery duels between the Federal forces in Fort Pickens and ships in the bay with the Confederate forces in Forts Barrancas and McRee began and continued off and on until the 24th. Neither side could claim victory, although the damage to the Confederate batteries was heavier. However, the duels demonstrated the strength of Fort Pickens and the power of the Federal forces to control the best naval base and harbor on the Gulf Coast, a position Union forces maintained throughout the war.

In the fall of 1861, the Confederate government stopped the policy of requisitioning the states and created military districts throughout the Confederacy under the command of military officers. Requisitions from the government were passed to the district commands, who would then seek aid from a governor in fulfilling the quota.

When Milton became governor of Florida, he began a program to reorganize the state militia. Perry had used the powers of military appointment to reward friends and had broken up regiments into companies in order to promote more officers of field grade. Milton reassembled the state forces of fourteen companies and placed four companies at Fernandina and nine companies at Apalachicola. At the same time, troops raised for transfer to the Confederate armies were equipped before being shipped to the poorly supplied Confederate forces.

Milton was concerned with the establishment of proper defenses at Apalachicola and St. Marks. Bragg had organized the area for defense with the forts in the Pensacola area. In East and Middle Florida, Milton hoped to repel Federal invasion through the use of fixed fortifications, which were to be strengthened from the rear with infantry and artillery forces. Milton considered the use of cavalry as a coast defense to be useless and expensive, and he emphasized the need for batteries with heavy guns at important points and gunboats with lighter fire power to guard between such points.

In the early months of the war, the Confederate government planned to defend the approaches to Apalachicola, the harbor and railroad terminus at Fernandina, the port of Jacksonville, and the port and navy yard at Pensacola. Munitions and troops were dispatched to these points. Cedar Key and all other towns on the coast were left undefended. Even at the towns to be defended, military supplies were woefully short.

But by February 1862, the pressure of Federal forces in Tennessee and Kentucky brought a sweeping order to the Florida departments to withdraw all men and supplies northward to defend the northwest border of the Confederacy. By the middle of April, only 1,500 Confederate troops remained in the Pensacola area, and, a month later, there were but 1,000 men left in the eastern and middle sections of the state. Coast defenses were generally dismantled, and military ordnance was moved into the interior.

Milton reflected the temper of Floridians when he wrote the Confederacy had abandoned most of Florida to the mercy and abuse of the Lincoln government. The seriousness of the Confederate situation was revealed when the Conscription Act was passed on April 16, 1862.

The evacuation of the troops from the coast defenses of Florida fitted in well with the plan of the Federal Navy Department to extend control southward along the Atlantic seaboard and around the Gulf Coast. By November 1861, the Federals held Port Royal, South Carolina. The next logical step would be the investment of Fernandina in the movement toward Key West and the strengthening of the union blockade.

During the war, Key West served as a nerve center for the intelligence services of both armies. Whites and blacks with Union leanings entered the town. Confederate sympathizers on the island served as liaison contacts for the forwarding of information to their beleaguered comrades.

When information reached Key West that Cedar Key, the Gulf terminus of the Florida Railroad, lacked the defense of either materiel or manpower, the USS *Hatteras* landed sailors and marines on January 15, 1862. The Federals found the town deserted and proceeded to burn eight loaded schooners and sloops, the railroad depot, freight cars, and a warehouse filled with naval stores. In addition, all telegraph lines were brought to the ground.

At the end of February, a Federal invasion force of eighteen gunboats and armed transports, six steamers, and eight sailing craft left Port Royal for the invasion and investment of East Florida. On March 3, the task force approached Amelia Island just as the last Confederate train crossed the trestle to the mainland.

According to one account, the town of Fernandina was virtually abandoned by troops and residents. On the last train, Yulee witnessed gunboat fire which pierced his car, fatally wounding the man by his side.

Colonel Edward Hopkins, Amelia Island's commander, was reported to have become ill at the Fernandina defenses. As a result the few guns and other munitions that were present were withdrawn. The residents left the town in disorder, and the remaining troops fled in retreat. The Federal forces occupied the town, and Amelia Island was returned to the jurisdiction of the United States.

On March 8, a task unit of gunboats, launches, and a transport sailed from Fernandina for Jacksonville and St. Augustine. On the night of the 11th, several hundred irregular Confederate troops, warned of the Federal advance, arrived in Jacksonville with orders to burn and destroy any property which might be of value to the enemy. These irregulars set the torch to sawmills, warehouses, machine shops, railroad buildings, business houses, and even private dwellings.

When the invaders arrived the following day, most of the town of Jacksonville was a shambles as the irregulars had plundered the establishments not destroyed by fire. A meeting of Unionists was held, and a premature political reconstruction was undertaken in the creation of a local government, which fell as soon as the Federals withdrew in April.

The Federal occupation of St. Augustine took place on March 11, 1862. Federal officials were escorted from the wharf to the town hall, where the mayor and council formally surrendered the town. About one-fifth of the 2,000 inhabitants left town on the approach of the Federal warship. The small Confederate garrison retired into the interior the night before.

The naval commander who accepted the surrender wrote:

> *I believe many citizens are earnestly attached to the Union, a large number silently opposed to it, and a still larger number who care very little about the matter. I think that nearly all the men acquiesce in the condition of affairs.*

By April 1862, the Federal forces controlled the East Coast from the St. Marys to St. Augustine, but the Confederate forces had only fallen back to Baldwin, twenty or thirty miles from the coast. Irregular troops and bushwhackers moved at will in the interior of the state, and most of the native population had gone inland to avoid the Federal invasion.

At this time, the Gulf Coast region from Pensacola though Cedar Key still remained in Confederate hands. The region had suffered several invasions, though the Federals were forced to withdraw. As on the East Coast, the continued withdrawal of troops for service on the Confederate northern front exposed the Gulf Coast to the sporadic raids of the ships of the Federal blockade.

On April 2, Apalachicola was occupied by a small force of Federal marines and sailors. To the conquerors, the town presented a desolate appearance. The batteries were dismantled; the warehouses and shops were closed; the streets and wharves were deserted, and the harbor was empty of ships. Perhaps 500 people out of a population of 2,500 remained. Those left behind were mostly poor whites and free Negroes. Destitution was apparent – no flour, no sugar, no meat, and very little corn. The people were dependent on fish and oysters for subsistence.

The work of destruction in extreme West Florida began on March 11 and continued through May 10. Saw mills, lumber stores, warehouses, naval stores, boats and gunboats, forage, food supplies, and clothing not absolutely essential to the civilian population were all burned or sabotaged. Munitions and machinery from the naval yard that could be removed were sent north to Alabama. Even the railroad leading out of Pensacola was ordered torn up and the bridges burned.

At midnight on May 9, the final preparations were completed and Pensacola was evacuated. All day, people had been leaving the city by all available means. Crowded trains had borne away the families whose homes had to be abandoned. Frightened children bewildered by their strange surroundings clung, weeping, to mothers or nurses almost as bewildered as themselves. Notice had been short, and little was clear except that by the inexorable decree of war all that stood for security and comfort had to be left behind.

At the last moment, the navy yard, the steamers, and the public buildings were set on fire, and the beautiful bay glowed with the flames. The Federal guns at Fort Pickens tried in vain with a fierce cannonading to prevent the Confederates from carrying out their plan. When all was finished, the last troops moved out; and the last strong position on the Florida coast was lost.

On May 10, the town was abandoned to Federal forces. Thus, Key West, Fernandina, St. Augustine, and Pensacola were returned to the Stars and Stripes after but little more than one year under the Stars and Bars.

The fate of Jacksonville, however, was to play the rope in a tug of war between the Federals and the Confederates. The town was occupied in March 1862 to establish Federal domination and, perhaps, to give aid to the Union sympathizers was evacuated less than a month later. No adequate explanation for the departure was ever given, but the Federal evacuation crippled the loyalists of whom some fifty or sixty went to New York City. The public press took up their case so pathetically that the city council voted $1,000 for their immediate relief."

The Federal blockade of the St. Johns River was maintained by gunboats of the South Atlantic Squadron, which had its station at Mayport Mills (a steam sawmill), a settlement that has continued in the present town of Mayport. The Federal gunboats patrolled the river to Jacksonville and beyond at will. To prevent the Federal patrols from reconnoitering up the St. Johns, Finegan, in command of the Confederate forces in East Florida, fortified St. Johns Bluff. Four miles above Mayport, as the river runs, the bluff was ideal for the purpose – a steep promontory rising from the river's edge to an elevation of more than seventy feet, the channel of the river running close inshore at that point.

By September 9, Finegan's forces had fortified the bluff and, at about the same time, a slave, who had sought the safety of the Federal lines, informed the gunboats at Mayport Mills of the Confederate maneuver. From September 10 through 30, the Federal gunboats sought to dislodge the cannoneers on the bluff without success, which forced the Federals to dispatch four transports and 1,600 men to the area for a joint sea and land attack. Under convoy of six gunboats, the task force moved into the river on October 1.

The Confederate scouts magnified the Federal strength into a force of 3,000 men, and as the Confederate forces only approached 600, an orderly retreat was ordered on October 2. The Federal forces razed the abandoned fortification the following day, and, on October 5, continued to Jacksonville.

Shortly after landing, a detachment of Confederate cavalry attacked the Federal pickets. Captain Valentine Chamberlain of the 7th Connecticut wrote:

> ...the outpost fired and fell back on the reserve. How the Seceshes did yell. I looked for them to come through the small timber. I heard one of my sergeants calling me; I looked behind and saw the captain in command of the 47th New York falling. I at first supposed him shot, but he had only fainted. He was quite frightened and had never been in any muss before. The Confederates were repulsed, but not before the rebel yell had felled one Union captain!

The next morning Chamberlain observed:

> ...that it was a gala time with the boys before the general found out what was going on, almost every store and shop on the street was broken into. Most of them had been closed for a long time, but there were goods in a few. A drug store was the best place. The boys pulled everything open and such a medley as they brought away. You can imagine, perhaps, a drug store, with most of the articles packed, opened, and overhauled by soldiers, who returned to their bivouac with their plunder... The general soon put a stop to most of this indiscriminate plundering.

A company of soldiers and two gunboats made a sortie up the river in search of Confederate steamers and to get the bounties of some Union men. Federal substitutes, who had agreed to serve in the army for someone else, were paid a bounty. When these soldiers deserted, a new activity was born. Men were sent out to catch the deserters and return them to military service or retrieve the bounty that they had been paid, thus the term, bounty hunter.

After ruthless raiding and burning along the banks of the upper St. Johns, the expedition captured the eighty-five foot steamer *Governor Milton* in a creek above Lake George. The soldiers returned with this booty as well as some Unionists. In a few days, the Federals left Jacksonville with some white and black refugees for the garrison at the St. Johns Bluff. Both the river and the town could be occupied at any time.

In March 1863, Federal troops returned to Jacksonville a third time. William Watson Davis, a student of the period, wrote in his book, *The Civil War and Reconstruction in Florida*:

> They came to collect Negro recruits, to plunder, and probably to inaugurate some vague plans of loyal political reconstruction.

The Federal forces were comprised of two regiments of Negroes under Colonel Thomas W. Higginson and reinforcements from the 6th Connecticut and 8th Maine.

The Federal troops pitched their camps in the town and occupied much of their time in conducting raids into the rural areas of the vicinity in search of plunder and Negro recruits. The presence of black troops under Higginson so infuriated the Confederate cavalry that retaliatory forays were made on the Federal forces. A number of sharp guerilla battles ensued. Private homes were invaded and there was an unnecessary abuse of non-combatants. As both Negro slaves and plunder were scarce, the Federal troops evacuated the Duval County section at the end of March, but not before troops from New England again scoured Jacksonville for loot. They fired many buildings, including several churches. By April 2, at least a third of the town was in ashes as a result of the savage vandalism of the drunken and irresponsible Federal soldiers.

★ ★ ★

In the first two years of the war, eight infantry regiments and two cavalry regiments were formed in Florida. Virtually all of the men in the infantry regiments went into combat in either the western or northern theaters of action. As the Confederate government could not furnish equipment for the cavalry, only a few of the cavalry companies continued on duty through the war. Several companies of artillery were enlisted for duty with the Confederacy.

In the later years of the war, a number of other regiments and companies were formed. Approximately 15,000 Floridians saw service in the Confederate Army with some 5,000 casualties. In addition, 1,200 Floridians, not including Negroes, joined the United States Army. Florida troops were in action on all fronts from April 1861 at Pensacola through the memorable battles at Corinth, Shiloh, Yorktown, Seven Days, Second Manassas, Gettysburg, Vicksburg, Chickamauga, and on to the surrender of the armies of Lee and Johnston in April 1865.

# 6
## LIFE IN THE CONFEDERACY

From the inception of the Confederate States at Montgomery in February 1861, the relationship of the Southern government with the state was often strained to if not near the breaking point. Milton and other governors were forced to decide the obligation of the state to the national government. Milton's unswerving allegiance to President Jefferson Davis and the Confederacy gave the Jackson county planter-lawyer-governor a secure claim to the unique honor of the most loyal state executive.

Frank L. Owsley, student of Confederate and state relationships, laid heavy emphasis on the individualistic and independent states' rights governors as one of the major reasons for the collapse of the Confederacy: He said that if a monument is ever erected as a symbolic gravestone over the Lost Cause, it should have engraved upon it these words: Died of States' Rights.

In October 1861, Milton wrote fellow Floridian, Secretary of the Navy Stephen R. Mallory:

> In the present deranged state of affairs, I shall be inaugurated and enter upon the duties of Governor... with a heavy heart and a fearful apprehension of my inability to perform the duties of the office creditably and very usefully; but to the best of my judgment, I will encounter surrounding difficulties, resolved to place the state upon the best war footing...

Milton's most immediate problem was in the realm of finance. The tax collections of the state had never passed $140,000 in any one year, yet Perry and the 1861 Legislature had put the government almost $500,000 in debt as a result of the mobilization effort. The state fiscal agencies were so demoralized after secession that tax collections were suspended for 1860-1861. In the confusion of the times, the accounts were so poorly kept that Treasurer William W. Davis was even unable to estimate with accuracy how much was really expended and for what.

Within six weeks of Milton's inauguration, the legislature was convened in regular session. Milton refused to accept the dilatory tactics and special legislation of the legislature, which seemed to view the pending war and national emergency as a short term problem that would soon pass. In retaliation, the legislature, composed in great part of members belonging to the radical element of the Democratic Party, the Perry group, neglected many of Milton's recommendations for recruiting troops and arming them. Instead, the legislature passed laws to spend the state's money on building railroads throughout the state.

In December, the dissidents sought to curtail the chief executive's power by recalling the secession convention for further action. Milton had been a strong proponent of secession and was a member of the secession convention. William Lamar Gammon, Milton's biographer, wrote that public opinion would not support a call for an election of a state convention which intended to reduce executive power to impotency. Thus, the reassembling of the old convention at the call of John C. McGehee, President of the Florida Secession Convention, was in order.

The convention assembled on January 14, 1862, in Tallahassee, and the attack on the governor's powers by the dissatisfied Democrats, now joined by several Constitutional Unionists, was underway. The state militia was abolished, an executive council to advise and approve the governor's action in militarizing the state was created, and anti-monopoly laws repealed before the assembly adjourned two weeks after of its commencement. Three members of the legislature, M.D. Papy, W.D. Barnes, and James A. Wiggins were appointed to the new executive council, but Milton's attacks on the council secured sufficient public support to abolish the council at the next session of the legislature. The vast majority of the population was solidly behind Milton and secession.

Among the other measures enacted at the 1861 and 1862 legislative sessions was an authorization for a county tax to be levied for the relief of the dependents of service men. Another measure allowed banks to suspend payments in specie from January 1862 until a year subsequent to the end of the war. This indefinite time was surely a result of the feeling that the war would very soon be over, and that the delay in payment would not be a lengthy affair. A fund of $25,000 was appropriated for the benefit of sick and wounded veterans, and the public domain, claimed by virtue of secession, was opened for sale at one to two dollars an acre, but service men were allowed a seventy-five percent discount from these prices.

In order to meet the increasing expenses of the war, the Confederate Congress ruled that planters should sell a set percentage of their produce to the government. Payment to the planters was made in Confederate bonds. In the vast areas now owned by the Confederate government and occupied by individuals, (areas for cattle grazing and timber) a direct war tax of $77,000 was imposed on the state. The property of those evading their share was made liable to confiscation by the state.

To offset the rigors of Confederate property impressments, the 1863 legislature sought to control Confederate government agents by civil law. A quota system for cotton and tobacco acreage was instituted in the hope that more land would be devoted to food crops.

One acre of cotton would be planted for each two hands owned or employed, and one quarter acre of tobacco per hand, except where the planter grew his own cotton or sold the same at prices fixed by the state or Confederate law. The use of grain, sugar or syrup in distilling was prohibited, and all distilleries were ordered abated as nuisances. For the purchase of clothing for Confederate soldiers, $75,000 was appropriated from the Florida treasury.

In addition to the confiscations by the Confederate government, the state confiscated where possible the property of persons continuing allegiance to the United States.

The final session of the 1864 legislature created special courts in each county to expedite the trial of an increasingly large number of Negro cases. With the continued Federal victories in the last months of the war, there was a mounting restlessness among the Negroes and a consequent increase in crime. The state militia was reconstituted and included all able-bodied men between sixteen and fifty-five with but few exempted classifications.

Resolutions against the denial of the civil liberties of civil trial, habeas corpus, free speech, jury trial, and the independence of the judiciary were passed by the two houses along with a resolution reaffirming the allegiance of Florida to the Southern Cause, along with a declaration that annihilation was preferable to a reunion with the United States.

By far, the most important work of the legislature, however, was in the field of financing Florida's part in the struggle for Southern independence. The extraordinary circumstances of war brought a complete revision of the state's fiscal arrangements. In February 1861, the legislature authorized an issue of $500,000 in state treasury notes, and the sale of twenty year bonds bearing an interest rate of eight percent.

During the same session, a number of banking and business corporations were chartered, and five existing banks received authority to increase capitalization provided that the money was paid into the state treasury, while the state pledged lands in the public domain as collateral for the stockholders.

Sensing the all important need of sustaining the value of state Treasury notes, legislators decreed that the circulation of solvent banks which received these state notes at par would be received at full value for all taxes. State taxes on such banks were suspended. Banks not accepting the state notes at par were forbidden to issue notes of less than $20 value.

Currency in circulation in the first year of the war was mainly in banknotes, state treasury notes, and the small change bills of railroads and other large corporations. In December 1861, bank note circulation reached $115,000 backed by $55,000 in specie. In 1862, Confederate money reached Florida, and since state treasury notes were backed by public lands, the Confederate notes were used to pay taxes and purchase state lands. In 1862, fractional notes of five to fifty cents were authorized by the legislature, and Tallahassee and Pensacola quickly put the small change notes in circulation.

After 1862, public finance in Florida was largely based on the note issues of the Confederacy and the state. Bank notes disappeared as the cheaper money came in full flood. Authorized state treasury note issues of seceded Florida reached $2,450,000; $1,800,000 of these notes was outstanding in May 1865. These obligations had been authorized by the Florida legislature. At the end of the war, the bank notes were rendered worthless.

Of the $500,000 bonds printed, $300,000 was sold. After the war, State Treasury notes and bonds were necessarily repudiated as part of an illegal debt. In 1864, as Union forces closed in on the lower South, inflation and hard times forced State Treasury notes out of circulation in favor of the heavily discounted paper notes of the Confederacy. At the end of the war, the war debt of Florida totaled $2,100,000.

The annual expenditures of the state in the war years averaged $500,000 divided between supplies for state troops, the Confederate direct tax of 1861, relief for dependents of servicemen and indigents and hospital care for Florida veterans, both in the state and the other Southern states.

Confederate taxes, in addition to that of 1861, were the Impressments Act and the General Tax Act of 1863. Under the former, Confederate agents seized food and other products for the armed forces at prices arbitrarily set by properly constituted boards. Impressed goods were either shipped to disposal points elsewhere or warehoused in depots established in major cities and towns. The General Tax Act authorized levies of eight percent on many agricultural products, occupational licenses from $50 to $500, fifteen percent tax on all incomes, ten percent profits tax on many commodities, and a further tithe tax of ten percent of all agricultural products.

The operation of the Confederate Impressments Act of 1863 served to engender resentment at first and then evasion and profiteering later. A similar law had existed in Florida for some time, but as the enforcement had been left to the local county commissioners, the element of cooperation had encouraged planters and farmers.

Under the Confederate law, agents, often unknown locally, alienated the local citizenry with brusque and high-handed action. Milton never approved of the impressments law, and, in at least one case, interfered with the work of the agents.

In 1863, Yulee sought relief through the Court after agents impounded 50,000 pounds of sugar from one of his plantations. Yulee had sold the sugar for a dollar a pound, and the sugar was in transit to its new owner when Confederate agents seized the shipment. Although the disputed commodity was sent on to the armies, Yulee contested the act, and the Confederate government was ordered by the Florida Supreme Court to give Yulee just compensation.

Considerable dishonesty was practiced by itinerant merchants, who posed as impressments agents. In addition, the swarm of independent government agents invited illegal impressments and, as ever, some citizens were shamelessly involved with the agents not only in speculation in food but also speculation in State and Confederate monies.

The railroad controversy between the officials of the Florida Railroad and the Confederate government over the impressments of iron rails from the roads in East Florida continued until the end of the war. The Confederate War Department ordered the tracks of the Fernandina-Baldwin and Jacksonville-Baldwin roads removed in order to extend rail connections westward to the Chattahoochee River. Both Finegan and Yulee opposed the removal of the iron and sought relief in civil court.

The fight assumed a sectional aspect when rumors spread that the interests of East Florida were to be sacrificed for those of Middle and West Florida. Confederate engineers charged with the removal of the tracks ignored the courts' injunction to stop the removal of the tracks. The operation continued but with much bitterness.

★ ★ ★

The United States Navy was called upon to establish a blockade of all southern Atlantic and Gulf ports and several blockading squadrons were formed.

In the first year of the war, a business was quickly established wherein certain vessels received clearance papers from both Confederate customs and the United States military officials. These ships were allowed to export cotton, naval stores, and tobacco. Their intended destination was to be ports in the United States and, in exchange, they could return with non-military cargos. Even though they had bonded themselves to the commitment of non-military cargos, this was soon brought to an end when merchants diverted their cargos to Europe and returned with weapons and other military items needed for the Confederacy.

In March 1862, a ship landed at New Smyrna, unloaded her cargo on the beach, and departed before capture by Federal ships. A second ship made the inner coast of Saint Andrews Bay and unloaded munitions for Florida and the Confederacy. Milton sent a force of 200 wagons to the east coast to secure the munitions brought through the blockade.

The excitement which prevailed with the arrival of the CSS *Florida* in Bear Creek was remembered by Catherine Cooper Hopley, an English tutor on Governor Milton's plantation, Sylvania, in Jackson County.

> Our boys did set off in double quick to the bay, to protect the valuable cargo, which, with the assistance of many citizens and their wagons within eighty miles, was brought safely to the Arsenal. Though within reach of the Yankees, they had labored unmolested, and the Marianna Dragoons came back quite disappointed at such an unaccountable fact.
>
> The Florida brought some other useful articles besides muskets; which for a time occupied all the ladies, and all their horses and carriages within many miles, as they seized the opportunity of making purchases until the new stock was (sic) quite exhausted.
>
> For some weeks cotton bales were being conveyed across the country to reload the Florida which, although she had got safely into port, was not allowed to escape again; but the shrewd Yankees had prudently determined to capture not only the ship, but her cargo of cotton too, and had postponed their attack until her rich freight presented a more tempting prize.
>
> Half the crew volunteered to go with the captors... but the pilot would not surrender, nor accept a bribe of $500 dollars to guide the ship out of Bear Creek. The consequence was she ran aground, and had to be lightened of a large portion of her cotton bales, which floated up the stream again, to the infinite amusement of the inhabitants.

As the war continued, and Federal forces strengthened the blockade, dwindling supplies and increased demand encouraged the blockade runners to import cargoes of consumer goods, which could be retailed at exorbitant prices when transported into the interior of Florida, Georgia, and Alabama. The easy money, though made at great risk, to be gained encouraged numerous Confederate officials to engage in the traffic, even to the extent of selling the imported goods at profitable rates to their own government.

Milton wrote in October 1862 that salt was selling at ten dollars per sack on first arrival of the blockade runners, but as soon as Confederate Quartermaster A.G. Sumner arrived, things changed, and salt was sold at thirty dollars per sack and at even fifty dollars in other localities.

The high profits to be realized from blockade running were reflected in the prices received for the smuggled goods. Miss Hopley wrote that:

> ...medicines, there were none of any consequence. Stimulants there were none... without mustard, black pepper, and many other trifles (red pepper is indigenous) – we often had no rice... no white sugar, very little molasses (an every day item of consumption), no more tea, and no more imported fruits. The cook was limited in her baking for want of soda, so largely used in the breads; Mrs. Milton was in perpetual dread of illness on account of the scarcity of medicines. Quinine, $20 an ounce; castor oil, $20 a gallon... a reel of cotton, half a dollar; common cotton cloths... half a dollar a yard; children's shoes, and very inferior ones, from three dollars upwards; full-sized shoes from five to ten dollars a pair; and other things in proportion.

At the same time, blockade runners were purchasing rum at seventeen cents a gallon in Cuba, according to Finegan, and selling the beverage inside the blockade for $25 a gallon.

Although the blockade running enterprises were lucrative and probably prostituted the honesty of many persons, the trade was a very necessary evil. As the states were charged with some responsibility in supplying the wants of citizens and soldiers, the blockade became a vital source of arms, munitions, and medicines.

In a letter written August 1862, Milton strongly condemned:

>...*the villainous traffic which is carried on by speculators under the plea of furnishing the people of the South with the prime necessities of life... In November last... five vessels were permitted to leave port and were captured by the enemy in transit. Since then, other vessels have left our ports with cotton, some of which have returned with coffee, salt, and other articles of merchandise, which the owners or their agents have disposed of at most exorbitant prices to the citizenry of this and adjacent states. Some of the goods were manufactured in the United States, and over the manufacturers' stamps upon the goods the names of English manufacturers were stamped, which, upon being removed, exhibited the cunning device of Yankee villainy, thus confirming the suspicion which I had entertained and expressed that frauds were perpetrated under the pretense of loyalty to the South.*
>
>*After patient inquiries of several months, the evidence obtained satisfied me beyond doubt that individuals residing in New York, Boston, Havana, and Nassau, and in some of our Southern cities, had formed co-partnerships by which to carry on the most nefarious and profitable traffic under false pretenses – partners residing at the South professing loyalty to the South, partners residing at the North professing loyalty to the North, and partners at intermediate points loyalty only to circumstances. The owners or agents in Havana or Nassau receive merchandise sent*

*from Northerns, and received also cotton shipped from the Southern ports – the merchandise to be sent to the Confederate States, the cotton to the United States – and thus the people, North and South, were and are fleeced by speculating traitors. By such base means our citizens have been and are subjected to the vilest system of extortion for the "prime necessities of life," and not only has cotton been thus obtained by the enemy, but information prejudicial to our interest has been obtained, our slaves have been corrupted and decoyed off, and some of the more ignorant portions of our white population made disloyal by the influence of our traitorous speculators.*

Despite the continuing protests of Milton, the Confederate government encouraged the blockade runners. It was not until 1864 that the Congress finally enacted legislation which sought to reserve space on the blockade runners for the exclusive use of the Confederacy. The reluctance of the government to regulate the traffic stimulated many farmers to increase cotton acreage in order to raise the money to purchase goods smuggled through the blockade. On occasions, when real necessities were landed, the officials were unable to secure drayage as the blockade runners could easily outbid the agents for the available wagons and teams.

★ ★ ★

One of the articles necessary to man's existence, which was sorely affected by the war and blockade, was salt. The insignificant commodity assumed an extraordinary importance when the usual sources of supply were cut off. During the war, salt became an element of primal concern. As Florida was a principal source of meat for the Confederacy and salt was a necessity for the preservation of slaughtered stock, the production of salt received increasing public and private attention. With the long coastlines, indented by bays and bayous, and sea water of high brine content, it was natural that salt-making became a major industry in Florida. This was especially true on the Gulf Coast from the Manatee section to Pensacola Bay, although the industry flourished on the sandy shores of Taylor County and St. Andrews Bay to a greater degree than elsewhere.

By the fall of 1862, the salt works along the Gulf Coast became the object of naval attacks, which continued until the fall of the Confederacy. In 1863, the salt enterprise of the Confederate government on the west arm of St. Andrews Bay was producing four hundred bushels of salt daily. The works, valued at half a million dollars, constituted a village of some twenty-seven buildings covering three-fourths of a square mile, and kept many hundred ox and mule teams constantly employed in hauling salt to Montgomery.

On December 10, Federal naval forces destroyed the installation. By the end of 1863, the losses in salt, salt works, wagons, boats, kettles, and boilers were estimated at over six million dollars. But no sooner had the Federal naval forces destroyed the works than the industry rose again, phoenix-like, from the ashes.

A large proportion of the works were located in the isolated marshes along St. Andrews Bay as the continued drought in that region, protracted through three years, had caused the evaporation of nearly all the fresh water. The water tested at least seventy-five percent salt. In addition, the quality of the salt was high, and large supplies of wood in the vicinity were available for firing the kettles.

The price of salt varied in the closing years of the war from twenty-five dollars a bushel to ninety dollars a barrel and later a dollar a pound. Planters boiled the dirt of smokehouse floors on which brine had dripped for years. When this supply was exhausted, planters in the Tallahassee area visited the Gulf Coast and placed large kettles in brick or clay furnaces, which were usually located several hundred feet from the tide line. Very near the furnace and kettles, a shallow well was dug, which always produced a plentiful supply of salty water. The salt water was boiled when there was only a thick brine left in the kettle. The brine was usually placed on clean boards for the drying and bleaching process.

The Confederate government, occupied with the war in the Border States and farther south in later years, did but little to protect the salt-makers. The coastal raids were conducted by Federal marines and sailors from the ships of the blockading squadrons, usually with less than 200 men. The importance of salt-making was sufficient to cause the men involved in the process to be exempt from compulsory service in the army. However, troops were never spared to protect this vital industry.

Insofar as industrial production affected by the war is concerned, the story of salt-making is indicative of manufacturing on the home front. During the war, Florida had imported all manner of manufactured goods before the war, goods and commodities were home-made generally or not at all. Stores sold their stocks and either closed out or reduced operations. Monticello became the lone seat of manufacturing with a small cotton mill, a wool-card factory, and a shoe factory.

General William Bailey, the proprietor of the cloth mill, kept his prices down and devoted the output to supplying the needs of Florida troops and alleviating the distress of poor families. He sent bales of yarn and cloth to the most interior counties to be distributed to true needy people. He estimated in June 1864 that he had foregone profits of at least $300,000 by pursuing this policy, Milton stated at the same time the state could purchase supplies from the mill at fifty percent less than the prevailing prices.

★ ★ ★

The status of agriculture during the war is not easily determined. While crops of corn, cane, peas, and potatoes were cultivated for home consumption, and some cotton and tobacco were in production, in 1864, the chief of the Confederate Commissary for

Florida stated that agriculture was on the decline. With thousands of men in the armed forces, most of them previously connected with agriculture; there is little reason to doubt the statement.

The importance of Florida as one of the food baskets of the Confederacy had been established in the early months of the conflict. In South Florida, on the prairies of the Kissimmee Valley and along Peace Creek, the ranchers were able to supply cattle for beef, tallow, and hides for Confederate forces. By 1864, Florida beef was the sole source of meat rations for Bragg's Army of Tennessee, and Beauregard's army that was at Charleston the Georgia and South Carolina supplies having been practically exhausted.

Professors Alfred Jackson Hanna and Kathryn Abbey Hanna authors of *Lake Okeechobee* (He was professor of history at Rollins University and she was the chair of the History Department at Florida State University) found in their study of Kissimmee-Okeechobee-Everglades watershed that in 1861, Jacob Summerlin, regarded as the cattle king of Florida, was reputed to be yearly breeding several thousand head of stock. Under overseer Sam Merlin's supervision, 600 head of cattle a week made the forty day drive from the Okeechobee-Kissimmee region to the railhead at Baldwin.

The herders started at dawn, rested the steers during the hottest hours of the day, and continued in the cool evening. They operated under constant pressure, for delivery was usually possible only from April to August. High water in the fall prevented starting the trail in South Florida while winter cold destroyed forage at the other end. The animals averaged almost 700 pounds when they started. By the end of the trek they had lost about 150 pounds.

Between 1861 and 1863, Summerlin was reported to have sold the Confederacy 25,000 steers at $8.00 a head. In 1863, Major Pleasant W. White was appointed as Florida's Commissary General. He centralized the collection of foodstuffs. White divided the state into districts placing Captain James McKay of Tampa at the head of the

South Florida district. McKay was the proprietor of several vessels that had been engaged in the Florida-West India trade. Under McKay's able direction, the cattle drives continued to the end of the war.

In 1864, General John K. Jackson reported that the most valuable portion of Florida was the middle counties of the Peninsula – Alachua, Marion, and other counties in the vicinity. Its productive capacity was very great, and the character of its supplies of inestimable value to the Confederacy. The sugar and produced cannot be supplied by any other portion of the Confederacy. From official and other data, Jackson learned that the production of army supplies amounted to 25,000 head of beeves, 1,000 hogsheads of sugar; 100,000 gallons syrup, 10,000 hogs, 50,000 sides of leather, 100,000 barrels of fish (if labor is available), oranges, lemons, arrowroot, salt, blockade goods, and iron, etc., annually. Counting the bacon at one-third pound and beef and fish at one pound to the ration, there were of meat rations of 45,000,000 – enough to supply 250,000 men for six months.

Florida's part in feeding soldiers, a prime necessity to military success as Napoleon aptly pointed out, assumed larger proportions in the closing years of the war. Both Confederates and Federals realized the heavy stakes involved in this battle of supply, a fact that was made eminently apparent at the largest battle fought in Florida, Olustee in 1864, when Federal forces were defeated in their one major attempt to cut this vital Confederate lifeline.

Florida's economic productivity was closely connected with the Confederate demands for manpower for the army. The first conscription act, passed in April 1862, sought all able-bodied men between eighteen and forty-five, but as time passed, other acts widened the age limits to those between fifteen and fifty. Even these later limits were disregarded as boys of fourteen and many men well past fifty volunteered for service. By 1864, practically all men able to bear arms were either in the Confederate service or organized into the militia of the home guard. The drainage of manpower was recognized in the enrollment of 17,000 names in the Confederate armies from Florida, and 1,290 whites and 1,044 blacks in the Union army.

Thousands of small farmers and dozens of overseers left farms and plantations without able directorship. Many men in the lower economic brackets accepted the role of serving as substitutes for men whose pocketbook could afford the annual $1,000 to $5,000 price tag. Milton inferred that such men slept every night in their own beds and bragged about state rights, out of danger's way, yet ever able to express their knowing opinion on the trouble with the war effort.

There was a scramble for substitutes or for the exempted positions in civil government, or as preachers, physicians, and teachers and as skilled laborers, overseers, or salt-makers. As an adherent of the doctrine of States' Rights, Milton believed the practice of conscription was abhorrent, but he was willing to waive the issue in view of the death struggle in which the Confederacy was involved. He urged Floridians subject to conscription to offer their services as volunteers.

In comparison with the other Confederate states, the number of men exempt from military service in Florida was very small. In 1865, the number of official exemptions was less than 750: 237 were physically disabled, 153 overseers, 152 railway employees, 120 public officials, and twenty preachers. The men of Florida, in general, overwhelmingly responded to the call to defend the state and the new nation. It was not until the last two years of the war, when defeat seemed inevitable, that there was any real opposition to the Cause or much desertion from its standards.

✯ ✯ ✯

Life on the home front during the four years of the war changed gradually from the rebellious joy at the time of secession to bleak despair with the surrender of General Robert E. Lee in April 1865. In many of the towns, the scene suddenly changed. In Pensacola, the situation changed from one seething with military and civil activities to one of desolation and destitution. The town appeared to be deserted. Grass grew in the street, and everything wore a sad and forlorn appearance.

After the original excitement subsided, and the troops began leaving the state, more and more attention was devoted to the collection of various materials, in short supply, for use in the Confederate war effort.

The limited resources of the Confederate government made the clothing and arming of troops difficult. The state government gave all that could be mustered and called upon the citizenry for assistance. Ellen Call Long recalled:

> Our women are most active and generous in lending their aid wherever needed. Many articles indispensable to the soldier are impossible to be purchased. Women have given carpets, piano-covers, blankets; all and everything that can be useful. Sewing societies have sprung up in every city, town, and hamlet. No moment is idle – in the cars traveling, visiting, in the dark and in the light, the knitting needle is going perpetually to clothe the feet of our soldiers. Many companies were uniformed by the sewing societies in cloth of homespun. Even the legislature, in a moment of extreme patriotism, passed a joint resolution to send the carpets, used at the Capitol, to be used by Florida troops in the field for any use they deemed necessary.

A plea to the patriotic women of Florida came on April 1, 1862. They were asked to donate what money, silver, and jewels they could. The *Florida Sentinel* noted that items donated included: five dollars and two silver forks; two dollars and one pair of sugar tongs; one fork, one spoon, and one napkin ring.

Catherine Hopley wrote:

> *At this time there was a perfect furore (sic) throughout the Confederacy for "Ladies, gunboat funds." Having supplied their soldiers with winter clothing and used up all the flannels, cloths, and wools that were then procurable, in adding to their wants, their attention has turned to the gunboats. In Charleston, Savannah, New Orleans, Mobile, and Richmond, as well as other places, ladies were forming societies for this object. One saw columns and columns of names and subscriptions acknowledged in the papers. Those who had money gave it, those who had not, gave plate and jewelry; the wealthy not only gave money themselves, but purchased, by raffling, the gifts of others, so that thus double assistance was rendered to the object.*

In the late spring of 1862, Beauregard issued what Hopley called:

> *...a beautiful and pathetic appeal to the country to spare their church and plantation bells to be molded into cannon. It is scarcely necessary to state it met with ready response. Mrs. Milton and all the people in our neighborhood had their old bells, copper kettles, brass door knobs, lead, and iron fragments collected and forwarded to Columbus, Georgia.*

The April 15, 1862 issue of the *Tallahassee Sentinel* reported a resolution that the Presbyterian Church offered their church bell, weighing 955 lbs., to the Confederate Government.

The people of Florida possessed a leader in Milton whom General J.B. Floyd called as noble a patriot as ever lived. To Milton, the war was personal and intimate. The governor's slaves were used to help build defense fortifications at no cost to the state, and he often paid the expenses of his aides while they were on state business. When he sent donations, he had collected for the hospital in Richmond for Florida soldiers, he often enclosed personal donations, sometimes as large as $1,000 and letters to be read to the sick and wounded about their homes.

The blockade resulted in many shortages of previously imported articles, but there was no serious discomfort in the interior sections where there were willing hands to make substitutes for articles that were no longer available. Tea, coffee, and white sugar virtually disappeared, although small supplies were hidden away for special occasions, for the sick, or to be sent to the soldiers' hospitals. As substitutes, roasted wheat, rye, or sweet potatoes served for coffee and yaupon or sassafras leaves were used for tea. Flour was imported from Georgia and Alabama in exchange for salt or fish. Even the task of preparing bread and cakes called for great ingenuity from the women. They found by grinding corn meal repeatedly followed each time by rigid sifting and then finally rubbing or pressing it through a course woolen blanket produced a soft light ingredient very similar to wheat flour in texture.

In the Manatee country, high prices and scarcity of money encouraged larger crops of corn and potatoes along with cotton patches. Spinning wheels were used to make thread, and some families had looms for weaving. Coloring of threads or homespun cloth was done with dyes made from the bark of hickory and mangrove trees. Cow, deer, and alligator hides were tanned and turned into shoes by cobblers in the community.

On plantations, the necessities of life were made by hand. Blacksmiths repaired tools, and those with a carpenter's bent fashioned articles from wood.

Homespun clothes, homemade shoes, hats of palmetto and cornhusks, homemade candles and soap, and other articles carried the people through. At Sylvania, when the hogs were slaughtered, one could not look out of a door or window without beholding cartloads of slaughtered pigs being carried to the yard to be cutup. All sorts of appendages were strung upon lines to be dried, and a whole row of Negroes were engaged in salting, packing, and drying these portions of pigs.

In the spring, the plums and watermelons furnished fruit and melons for those who cultivated them, while the abundance of vegetables brought ten or twelve kinds on the table at once, several of which, such as okra, are peculiar to the South.

Florida newspapers gradually dropped their advertisements as the advertisers went to war and the shortages of paper forced the reduction in size or, in the case of many papers, a suspension of publication. In every issue, newspapers carried recipes for the home manufacture of soap, dye, vinegar, candles, and salt. In view of the shortage of medicine, the papers carried lists of roots and herbs that were needed for the army medical services.

Army surgeons were badly handicapped by the lack of supplies. Quinine and morphine had to be smuggled through the Federal lines or the blockade.

In the spring of 1865, prices paid for commodities at the Lake City Hospital revealed the inflation of the times: Eggs, $2.50 per dozen; tin pans, $15 each; whiskey, $125 a gallon; vinegar, $5 a gallon; milk, $1 a quart; $6 for a bottle of ink; and $5 for a pound of butter.

★ ★ ★

One of the major problems on the home front arose during the very early days of the war and continued until the surrender. It dealt with the necessary provisions for the dependents of the service men. At first, the local citizenry tried to provide the support. Thus, when a volunteer company was formed at Pensacola, there was wanted twelve men who were required to make out the requisite number.

W.J. Norris was a resident of Bluff Springs and wished to join the Guards, but could leave no support for his family. Milton told him that if the relief committee did not provide for his family, he would see that they were cared for until other and sufficient provisions were made. Accordingly, Milton gave Norris' wife credit at the provision store at Bluff Springs, and she has got all that she called for.

When the Federal forces moved into Fernandina, Jacksonville, St. Augustine, and other settlements on the East Coast, most of the residents evacuated their homes and businesses and moved inland, where large numbers existed as refugees. Among these refugees were many soldiers' families.

Milton had promised to make provisions for the families of men leaving for the front. Through state action, supplies of corn, syrup, potatoes, and peas along with bacon, pork, and beef were procured and distributed to the soldiers' dependents. Nonetheless, if the few sources available are an indication of the contemporary situation, there were many soldiers' dependents who subsisted through the last years of the war on the ragged edge of existence.

The 1862 legislature appropriated $200,000 for the relief of the dependents of men in the armed forces, while the 1863 and 1864 legislatures increased the amount to $500,000 annually. In addition, the legislature provided for the purchase and distribution of cotton and wool-cards to be used in the home preparation of cotton and wool for spinning thread.

As residents of both coasts abandoned their homes in front of the advancing Federals and moved toward the interior, the problem of caring for the refugees complicated the housing and supply problems. With few possessions and fewer resources, there was much suffering. Many refugees settled with kin people, while others were taken into private homes. In addition, the refugees' slaves were moved to prevent their capture by Federal forces. Many slaves were transferred to plantations where their labor aided the production of foodstuffs and livestock.

The story of Margaret Fleming, mistress of Hibernia on the St. Johns, was but one of the thousands of heartache and suffering. When war broke out, her sons, Seton and Frank, volunteered at once. In 1862, Lewis Fleming, her husband, died, and a third son, Frederic, enlisted in the First Florida Cavalry at the age of fifteen. In 1863, William, her youngest son, enlisted at the age of thirteen.

In 1864, Margaret received news that Seton had been killed at Cold Harbor. The climax was reached when Margaret and her three little girls walked to Middleburg to flee the Federal advance.

From Middleburg, Margaret took her small brood to Lake City, where she worked in the hospital to lighten the ever-increasing suffering, giving what comfort and help she could in a world gone bleak and comfortless for so many.

As the war drew towards the end, there was much bitterness in the hearts of those who had lost husbands, fathers, and brothers in action. Grief stricken cries arose that the exempted serve in combat; that schools be closed, that there was a need for soldiers and fighters, not teachers and salt-makers. Hopley wrote:

> [Yet] *not all was sorrow for wedged in between these harsh and mournful occasions were little bits of joy and gladness inconsequential in scope, a husband home on furlough – a brother or sweetheart perhaps – a taffy pulling now and then a singing. Yes the people could still sing and every Sabbath found them faithful at the little church for worship. There were days of fasting and prayer. These were rigidly observed. People prayed that the terrible ordeal would soon be over.*

★ ★ ★

In the towns of the interior, there was still some social gaiety. The social tradition of the South, even in war-time, was such that parties and balls were often the order of the evening. When soldiers were in the community, the military prestige of the uniforms added to the glamour that could be produced under tallow candles, while dancing or partaking of such refreshments as could be conjured from behind the blockade. The ladies' dresses were remodeled from pre-war wardrobes and even dancing shoes were hand-made. For a little while, hearts were light – or seemed to be.

At Sylvania, the arrival of Milton's nephew, Major Milton Brown, from Texas, was the hour for great doings in the parlor. The piano gave forth the liveliest airs, while merry steps kept time to the music, and scarcely a day passed that some other cousin did not arrive to add to the group. The girls were all excellent musicians, and there were two good pianos in the house, often both in use at the same time.

On Christmas in 1862, a wedding at the glamorous Gamble Mansion in Manatee country was attended by most of the residents of that section. After the wedding and the wedding supper, the furniture in the dining room was cleared away for dancing. Henry Ware (Bud) was not yet of conscript age and was on hand as fiddler and prompter. Many of the guests, old and young, joined in the old square dance.

★★★

There remained but few schools by the end of the war. Milton was able to hire tutors for six of his ten school-aged children. The little Miltons along with several other children of the planters in the neighborhood attended school in a large room across the yard from the plantation house. Captain Archibald McNeill, deputy commissary agent for Manatee county, hired Flora Ellen McLeod to reside with his wife at Gamble Mansion as his wife's companion and teacher for their children. However, the schools and academies at Ocala, Micanopy, Monticello, and other towns closed in the early years of the war.

★ ★ ★

Although the burden of the war fell heavily upon the men in combat, many of whom never returned to their homes, a heavier burden fell upon those who not only gave their sons and husbands to the Cause but who stayed behind and kept the home fires burning. Not only did the women take charge of many of the farms and plantations, felled trees and rolled logs, cleared fields and planted crops, ploughed and hoed, besides weaving, sewing, and cooking, but they also lived out the dreary days and sleepless nights waiting for news from the front.

Milton paid homage to the women by saying that the brightest page in the future history of the Confederate States will distinguish the ladies of the South for their patriotism, courage, and energy.

Women joined in the efforts to establish hospitals at Lake City, Monticello, and Tallahassee. Moved by the sad condition of the Florida troops in the Army of Northern Virginia, Milton established a Florida Hospital in Richmond. Mrs. Martha M. Reid, widow of Governor Robert R. Reid, served as matron of the hospital, while Mrs. Elizabeth Harris served as superintendent of the hospital for the western army. The names of these ladies and others were held in reverence for their noble service to the sick and wounded. A ward in the Howard Grove Hospital in Richmond was also assigned for the Florida sick and wounded.

★ ★ ★

As the last year of the war slowly wore on, the strength of the Confederacy ebbed away. Corn, meat, and salt were scarce; livestock had been impressed for the army; grim desolation held the occupied areas. Each day brought new disaster; a century of sorrow was crowded into a year. The intermittent post brought news of death, death, death, until the very world seemed dying beneath the eyes of Florida's simple population. The women at home, sad-eyed and poverty stricken, waited for the nightmare of misery to end.

On a visit to the Whitaker homestead on Sarasota Bayou, predatory Union bushwhackers ransacked the place and called for matches to set the house on fire. Without arguing, Mary Whitaker went into the house and returned with a block of matches and with a calmness not altogether pretense, she handed it to the commanding officer and said, "Sir, I want to look into the eyes of a man who can stoop so low as to burn the home of a helpless woman and her children."

Without further thought, the Union men set fire to the house and watched as it burned to the ground.

★★★

Another segment of Florida society which, in its way, aided the Southern fight for national independence was the Negro. At the time of secession, roughly a half of Florida's population was composed of members of the black race of whom virtually all were slaves. At the outset of the war, many may well wonder why the slave population of the South did not seek its freedom as the white population was engaged in a war to the death.

The answer is generally found in the fact that slavery had become the greatest school for civilizing a race of barbaric savages that the world has ever known. From the day that the first African was introduced into North America, the education and training of the Negro in the culture and folklore of Western Civilization began.

Over the centuries, as new slaves were introduced into the American environment, this civilizing and educating process went on and was handed down from generation to generation, François

Louis Nompar de Caumont LaPort, Compt de Castelnau, a naturalist employed by the French government to study life in the Americas, visited the raw frontier of Middle Florida in 1838. He wrote down the slaves' comment on the free Negro: "Poor fellow," they say, "he has no master." The mass of the Southern slaves were well-fed, well-housed, well-treated, well-watched, and well-controlled. The mass of slaves were content. Edwin Percy Whipple, William Cullen Bryant and other northern visitors to Florida were convinced that, in reality, the master was the slave!

At the outbreak of the war, the slave patrol laws were strengthened, but by 1864, over four-fifths of the able-bodied white males were in the armed services so that the enforcement of the patrol was doubtful.

As it already has been pointed out, the very large majority of the slaves in 1860 were in the seven plantation counties, and none of these counties were invaded by the Federals until the last year of the war. The Federal occupation of the east coast from Fernandina to St. Augustine, Cedar Key, Tampa, Ft. Myers, and Pensacola on the Gulf Coast enabled some slaves to cross the Federal lines to freedom, but most of the slaves had been moved inland.

By the last year of the war, at Hibernia, there were fewer and fewer hands on the plantation, more neglected fields, fewer house servants. Yet when Frederic Fleming returned after the war, an old family slave, living in the quarters, was the first person to greet the ex-soldier. Hibernia had been built by George Fleming, who immigrated to Florida from Scotland in 1785. At the time of the war, Hibernia was the home of Francis Philip and Seton Fleming.

In the Manatee country, a number of Negro slaves were enticed away by Union sympathizers; but, in 1862, at Jacksonville, the Federal plan to secure slaves for black regiments was a failure.

The Negro troops which wore service uniforms in Florida were all members of companies recruited from former slaves in Florida and the other Southern states. The Confederacy was about to draft slaves when the war ended. There is no doubt that Federal raiding parties would have penetrated the interior areas of the state on protracted slave hunts had the Federals not been stopped by the cavalry of John Jackson Dickison in East Florida and the Cow Cavalry of Charles J. Munnerlyn in South Florida.

Within the areas occupied by the Federal forces, the presence of Negroes gave the Federals many opportunities to practice the program of freedom, which the abolitionists had been preaching during the ante-bellum years. In 1864, the Freedman's Aid Society, with help from the army, had opened common schools for the Negroes with women teachers from the North. At Jacksonville, the school was also open to white children, but by the end of the year the schools were closed.

After 1862, the problem of the legal status of the slaves of loyal Floridians as opposed to captured slaves was finally settled on the basis that slaves who belonged to the loyalists were still slaves; those of the disloyal were free captives of war when within the occupied areas. The Emancipation Proclamation which affected slaves in the rebellious states finally settled the meaning of this provocative question by confirming slaves belonging to Southerners in occupied areas were free, but people loyal to the Union could keep their slaves.

# PART II

## Battles and Raids Throughout Florida

# 7
## BATTLE OF PENSACOLA

Pensacola's history is closely tied to Pensacola Bay. Beginning in 1829, the government had built four major fortifications: Fort Pickens on Santa Rosa Island, Fort McRee (named after Major William McRee, one of the Army's first engineers) on the opposite side of the harbor entrance, Fort Barrancas on the mainland (currently located on the Naval Air Station in Pensacola) near the Navy Yard, and behind Barrancas, the Advanced Redoubt, which was completed in 1859.

Seacoast forts were generally so dominant that their presence was enough to discourage any conflict. It was generally unnecessary to station troops in the forts; therefore, most forts in the South were taken over by Confederate forces without a fight. The situation in Pensacola, however, was different. Federal troops were stationed in Pensacola with orders to defend the forts. Troops were moved from Fort Barrancas to Fort Pickens on January 10, 1861.

Confederate volunteers assembled in Pensacola. Two days after Florida seceded; the volunteers seized the Navy Yard and facilities on the mainland. They demanded the surrender of Fort Pickens, but Federal commander, Lieutenant Adam J. Slemmer, refused to surrender the fort as long as he could defend it.

A truce had been reached in Washington between William H. Seward (Senator from New York and Lincoln's nominee for Secretary of State) and Senator Mallory, who was destined to be the Confederate Secretary of the Navy. On January 29, President Buchanan issued orders to his Secretaries of War and the Navy:

*Upon receiving satisfactory assurances from Mr. Mallory*
*and Colonel Chase that Fort Pickens will not be attacked, you*

*are instructed not to land the company on board the Brooklyn unless said fort shall be attacked or preparations made for the attack.*

Federal reinforcements were sent from New York to Fort Pickens early in February. Since landing the troops would break the truce, the Federal forces remained offshore for ten weeks.

There were cannons at the fort's entrance, which were loaded and manned, but for the next several weeks, the agreed upon truce prevailed. As long as the Federal government did not reinforce Fort Pickens, the Confederates agreed not to attack the fort. Ships from Mobile and New Orleans continued to bring more Confederate forces to Pensacola.

Confederate General Braxton Bragg had been sent to Pensacola to take command. When Lincoln learned that Fort Pickens had not been reinforced, he sent Lieutenant John Warden, who later commanded the USS *Monitor* when it met the CSS *Virginia*, as his personal messenger. Warden traveled by train from Washington to Pensacola. He was allowed to pass through the lines and delivered Lincoln's message that reinforcements would be sent to Fort Pickens, thus violating the truce.

Although today's common wisdom tells us that the war started with the firing on Fort Sumter in Charleston Harbor, the truth of the matter is that the first blood shed in the war was in Pensacola Harbor when a small Confederate patrol boat was fired upon, wounding two sailors. Both Fort Sumter and Fort Pickens events were caused by the Federal government violating the agreed upon truces. However, Fort Sumter was larger, and the news from Charleston traveled faster than from Pensacola, so we accept Fort Sumter as the technical beginning of the war. Both of these events clearly prove that Lincoln wanted a war with the Confederacy.

The first reinforcements landed at Fort Pickens on April 13 at 2:00 a.m. This was done at almost the same time the truce was violated by Federal forces at Fort Sumter.

Even more reinforcements landed a few days later. Colonel Harvey Brown took command at Fort Pickens. Brown informed the troops that Fort Sumter had surrendered after a gallant defense and the war had begun. Fort Pickens was now a lonely outpost deep in enemy territory. In the months that followed, Bragg trained his recruits, and Brown built gun batteries around the fort.

In September, Brown tried to provoke Bragg into a fight. The first attempt was the burning of an expensive floating dry dock in the harbor. However, Bragg was unmoved, as he had been ordered not to attack the fort.

In full view of Federal forces, the Confederates began mounting cannons on a ship at the Navy Yard. On the night of September 13, about 100 Federal sailors and marines quietly rowed boats into the harbor, surprised the guards at the Navy Yard, and burned the Confederate ships.

Three Federal and three Confederate sailors were killed. Three weeks later, a force of over 1,000 Confederates attacked the Union camps outside Fort Pickens. On October 9, the battle of Santa Rosa Island was fought before dawn. The 6th New York Infantry's camp was destroyed before the Confederates were forced back to their boats.

Each side lost approximately sixty men in the fight. Now it was the Federals turn to respond. On November 22, at 10:00 a.m., a signal flag went up at Fort Pickens to alert the Navy. Cannons roared from the fort. Two ships fired at Fort McRee, and guns from Santa Rosa Island rained shot and shell all along the Confederate line to the Navy Yard.

The bombardment continued all day, resumed the next morning, and continued until midnight. Brown reported that about 5,000 shot and shell were fired by his guns and the Navy, and about 1,000 were fired from the Confederates. Houses were burned around the Navy Yard. Fort McRee was in ruins, while Fort Pickens and Fort Barrancas suffered less damage.

Casualties on both sides were light. The USS *Niagara* had one man killed and seven wounded. Fort Pickens suffered one killed and six wounded when an overheated cannon burst. Confederate losses were seven dead and twenty-one wounded. Windows were shattered in Pensacola, and thousands of dead fish floated on Pensacola Bay, victims of the terrific concussions.

Two days later, Federal losses climbed when two Confederate shells exploded while being removed from Fort Pickens. Five men were killed, and seven more soldiers were wounded in the explosions.

The Battle of Pensacola Bay was over. The Confederates withdrew from Pensacola on May 8, 1862, and Federal troops occupied Fort Barrancas and the Navy Yard the following day. Federal troops continued to occupy Pensacola until the end of the war. Fort McRee eventually collapsed into the sea, a casualty of the frequent hurricanes to hit the area. In 2004, Fort Pickens was severely damaged by Hurricane Ivan but has been reopened to the public. Both Fort Barrancas and the Advanced Redoubt are still standing.

# 8
## JACKSONVILLE AND THE SURROUNDING AREA

In 1860, there were only three communities that had a population of 2,000 or greater. Jacksonville was in third place barely reaching the 2,000 mark. Established on the St. Johns River, close to its mouth at the Atlantic Ocean, Jacksonville quickly became an important seaport.

It was written that as many as six large schooners would be tied up at Jacksonville wharfs taking on up to 100,000 feet of lumber. The timber and lumber industry had become the financial backbone of the area. Logs would be harvested upriver and floated downstream to Jacksonville, where sawmills would process them for shipment up north or to Europe. Cotton was also a major cash crop in central Florida. Middleburg had become an important inland port for the shipping of cotton via Black Creek to the St. Johns and on to Jacksonville for shipment to faraway ports. Schooners were limited to a ten and a half foot draft, as the St. Johns Bar would restrict passage.

★ ★ ★

Shortly after secession, the Jacksonville Light Artillery was mustered into the Florida Light Artillery and stationed on Amelia Island, Talbot Island, and at St. Johns Bluff. In November 1861, General Robert E. Lee, then head of the Department of South Carolina, Georgia, and East Florida, visited and inspected the installations. Lee told Brigadier General James H. Trapier, Commander of East and Central Florida, that the preparations were poor at best, and he truly hoped that the Federals would be polite enough to wait until the fortifications were strengthened before they attacked. Lee ordered the abandonment of Talbot Island and the strengthening of the Amelia Island and St. Johns River defenses.

In February 1862, Lee also told Trapier to remove the defenses from Mayport Mills and St. Johns Bluff to Yellow Bluff, but before this could be accomplished, the Federals arrived. The Confederates, severely outnumbered, abandoned these locations, leaving them in Federal hands for the remainder of the war.

The Confederates bought the USS *America* for blockade running, renaming her CSS *Camilla*. She was stationed at Jacksonville. Beginning in December 1861, she left port on at least two successful voyages.

On March 11, 1862, Federal gunboats and transports arrived at Mayport Mills. That night, Confederate forces withdrew from St. Johns Bluff to Jacksonville where they burned a nearly completed warship, seven sawmills, four million board feet of timber, two iron foundries, and the railroad depot. The Confederates sailed the *Camilla* to Dunn's Creek and scuttled her.

On 28 March 1862, Federal Lieutenant Commander Thomas Holdup Stevens wrote about raising the *Camilla*:

> *I returned this morning with the launch and the first cutter of the Wabash and the steamers Darington and Ellen from Dunn's Creek with the yacht America, which, after a week's hard labor and the valuable assistance of Lieutenant John Irwin, Acting Master William Budd, and First Assistant Engineer William W. Dungan, I succeeded in raising and bringing to this place, where I shall keep her awaiting your further instructions. She is without ground tackle or sails and almost everything else, but her lower masts, bowsprit, gaffs, and some light spars.*

Unbeknownst to Stevens, he and his crew were watched by Captain Winston Stephens and the men of the 2nd Florida Cavalry. Stephens, a native of Georgia who lived in Welaka, had joined the cavalry after receiving assurances that the 2nd Florida Cavalry would serve only as a home guard. Stephens had been ordered to Dunn's Creek to prevent the yacht from being raised. When he saw the sailors peacefully engaged in their work, Stephens lamented that he couldn't shoot them because it would be murder. He and his men returned to Welaka. Once raised, the yacht joined the Union's blockade squadron off Charleston, where she participated in the sinking of several Confederate blockade runners.

After Fernandina fell to Federal forces in March 1862, many residents of Jacksonville fled with their belongings to Lake City. There was never an organized defense of Jacksonville, and seeing no alternative, Jacksonville's Sheriff Frederick Lueders waved a flag of truce and surrendered the city to General Thomas W. Sherman.

Coming out of hiding were a group of citizens sympathetic to the Federal cause, led by Unionist Calvin L. Robinson. They visited Sherman on March 20 and requested he permanently occupy the city to insure their safety. On March 24, General H.G. Wright assumed command in Jacksonville, and the Unionists announced that a convention to create a loyal state government would meet on April 10.

The area surrounding Jacksonville was patrolled by Confederate cavalry, which made the small occupation force of 1,400 Federal soldiers very uncomfortable. They feared that an attack on their garrison could occur at any time. By coincidence, the Federals were all evacuated the day before the convention commenced. Jacksonville's Unionists used the evacuation to escape by departing on Federal transport vessels. As the Federal ships departed, a detachment of the Florida 1st Cavalry rode into town and watched the ships from a wharf.

Although the first occupation of the city had ended, Federal gunboats were continually patrolling the St. Johns River. Finegan ordered the construction of batteries at Yellow Bluff and St. Johns Bluff. On September 11, the St. Johns Bluff Battery opened fire on a Federal gunboat that had fired on the bluff the previous evening. The ensuing firefight lasted more than four hours. Stephens commented on the fight:

> *We have the game played out with the gunboats on this river... The second took place on the morning of the 17th at 5:00 a.m. and lasted till 10:00 p.m. In which time the gunboats threw as estimated between 1,000 and 1,200 shots, and our guns replied very slowly only throwing some shots. The boats then retired... The batteries received no injury during the firing, but the shell and shot fell like hail.*

These exchanges led to the reoccupation of the St. Johns. On September 30, four Union transports, under the command of Brigadier General John M. Brannon, landed at Mayport Mills. Confederate Lieutenant Colonel C.F. Hopkins, commander at St. Johns Bluff, requested reinforcements. Soldiers were sent from Yellow Bluff. The next morning, as Federal gunboats and infantry units advanced on the bluff, the 500 Confederate troops, knowing they lacked adequate manpower to defend Yellow Bluff, evacuated their defenses.

In Charleston , Beauregard, now commanding the Department of South Carolina, Georgia, and East Florida, ordered two regiments to Florida to save the St. John's River and perhaps East Florida.

Jacksonville was again invaded by Federal forces on October 5th. Two weeks later, the 8th Maine and 6th Connecticut and two regiments of colored soldiers, the 1st and 2nd South Carolina USCT, composed mostly of former slaves arrived and occupied the city.

It was Finegan's belief that the colored soldiers were sent to Florida to encourage the slaves to rebel. Confirming Finegan's suspicions, a Federal general wrote that the objective of Jacksonville's occupation was to make it the base of operations for the arming of Negroes and, in this way, securing possession of the entire state of Florida.

The Federal forces established themselves on the west side of present downtown Jacksonville and built Forts Higginson and Montgomery, which were named for the colonels commanding the colored troops. These forts were at the terminus of the Florida Atlantic and Gulf Central Railroad on the site of today's Prime Osborne Convention Center.

On October 9, Brannon, finding it impossible to destroy all of the corn fields along the river banks, left Jacksonville and withdrew to Hilton Head, South Carolina. Stephens was ordered to inspect the town, which he found vandalized:

> I went to Mrs. Maxey's house and everything was torn upside down, two trunks had been broken open and everything gone. I saw the picture Mother sent down for old Mother Bryant and gave it to Captain Michel to take care of until otherwise ordered. I saw some books with Mr. Tidings name in them, but everything but the furniture was carried off by the vandals and Negroes... Mrs. Foster said the chaplain of one of the Yankee Regiments did more harm in Jacksonville than anyone else, as he was an abolitionist and allowed negroes to take anything they claimed, no matter who they claimed it of.

On March 10, 1863, 1,400 Federal black troops under the command of white officers arrived and began building breastworks at key locations in Jacksonville. These included Forts Higginson and Montgomery.

Confederates were camped several miles west of the city and controlled the countryside. When the Federals would send out scouting parties, the Confederates would fire upon them, sending them back to the protection of the city and the naval guns in place there.

On March 17, Finegan requested the Federals send all women and children out of the town. Higginson provided wagons for noncombatants, who were met at the brickyard by Confederate escorts and taken to Lake City.

On March 25th, the Confederates mounted an eight inch rifled cannon on a rail car and brought it within firing range of the city. Seven rounds were fired before a Federal gunboat returned fire. The Confederates retired. The Federals mounted a four-inch gun on a hand railroad car. In retaliation, a working party took the car up track four miles from the city. The Confederates returned with their railcar cannon and opened fire, which caused the Federals to retreat. Four days later, the Federals withdrew from the city, but before departing, they burned numerous buildings, including St. Johns Church. Stephens described their actions:

*They destroyed many buildings in Jacksonville, but I am not familiar enough to repeat the names so that you can know whose houses they did burn. The block on which Mrs. Foster's house stood is destroyed; all but the house on the South West corner, the block north of that is destroyed, Pearson's houses are destroyed, the Catholic and Presbyterian churches are destroyed, Colonel Hart's building and brick office Bisher & Canova Store, and the one nearest I think Hickmans then Parkhurst stores, and the two brick stores on the corner next [to the] Ochus Hotel, and the shoe shop adjoining. Those are all the stores destroyed I think but in the vicinity of the dwelling of Col Harts place several houses are burnt, and in the other parts of the town. I forgot to say the Courthouse was destroyed... We saved Colonel Sanderson's house and some others that were on fire.*

The Confederates had developed torpedoes (known today as mines) and placed them in strategic locations in the river. The USS *Maple Leaf* hit a Confederate torpedo and sunk just off of Mandarin Point, which is on the southern edge of modern day Jacksonville. Other sinkings by mines included the USS *Alice Price*, a large Federal transport, which was sunk near Jacksonville.

The river war continued for the duration of the war. The St. Johns River was the Federal route of choice into the interior of Florida but was hotly contested by the Confederates. Company H of the 2nd Florida Cavalry led by Captain John J. Dickison was especially active in the interior defense. Several of Dickison's activities are covered elsewhere in this book.

In the fall of 1863, President Lincoln's reelection was anything but certain. The general sentiment was against the war as draft riots had occurred in many cities throughout the North. The Democrat candidate, General George McClellan, was running as the peace candidate. Clearly, Lincoln needed a victory or event to bolster his popularity and salvage his reelection. In correspondence with Major General Quincy A. Gilmore, commander of the Federal Department of the South, Lincoln referred to the need to invade Florida, cut off the Confederate food supplies, capture the Tallahassee and allow loyal Unionists resident have the state rejoin the Union. As this campaign was far removed from the thrust of the Federal war efforts, and tactically of no importance to the war effort, it can be presumed that Lincoln saw that such a successful campaign would strengthen his election chances.

★ ★ ★

On February 3, 1864, a flotilla of thirty-eight troop transports left the Federal base at Hilton Head, carrying over 7,000 soldiers, and steamed south. On February 7, 1864, these troops, under the command of Brigadier General Truman Seymour, arrived in Jacksonville.

From here, the Federal army was to set out westward in an expedition, but the Federals were not sure how to proceed. In Jacksonville, Gilmore met with Seymour, who was not convinced that an invasion into the interior was possible or would achieve the desired results. After several days of heated discussion, Gilmore told Seymour to remain in Jacksonville with his forces while Gilmore returned to his headquarters. Seymour must have suspected that Gilmore was going to replace him and decided, against current orders, to start the invasion. There is no other plausible justification for a general officer to disobey direct orders from his superior unless it was to save his career.

The Confederates reacted to this new threat. From Charleston, Beauregard had observed Federal ships leaving Hilton Head and traveled to Savannah in anticipation of an invasion there. When the invasion did not happen, he returned to Charleston. Before departing, Beauregard left orders that two infantry units and a light artillery battery be prepared to go to Florida on short notice.

These preparations were put to the test. Responding to Finegan's report of the Federal landing at Jacksonville, Beauregard directed that the troops on alert in Savannah move immediately to Florida. At the same time Brigadier General Alfred H. Colquitt's brigade of Georgians, which would also include the 1st Florida Special Battalion, were shifted from Charleston to Savannah and was prepared to move to Florida.

Finegan gathered up all of the available forces and concentrated them at Olustee about fifteen miles east of Lake City and forty miles west of Jacksonville. Colquitt's brigade, along with the others, all consisting of Georgia and Florida regiments, were also ordered to converge on Olustee.

This area is bordered on the north by the Okefenokee Swamp and to the south by water and more swamp. The only route the Federals could take was along the road and rail line that went west from Jacksonville toward Tallahassee. As the Union soldiers advanced, they were continually attacked by Confederate pickets, who would quickly retreat. Despite their success at dispersing Confederate pickets, it seems the Federal command was still frightened of ambush. Each time any Federal unit left the protection of the naval guns on the St. John's River, the unit was ambushed. It is natural to expect this concern continued when the troops headed west along the swampy areas which were home country to Confederate troops.

The apparent indecision and debate regarding the wisdom of the Federal invasion ate up twelve days, giving the Confederates time to pull together their limited troops from South Carolina, Georgia, and Central Florida on foot and over incomplete railroad systems. Finegan's engineers picked a defensible dry area along the railroad abutted by swamps and lakes. They dug in and prepared for the expected attack.

The Federals advanced along the Lake City and Jacksonville pike and the railroad track. Early in the afternoon of February 20, 1864, advance Federal cavalry skirmished with their Confederate counterparts. Like the pickets, the cavalry would retreat after the initial engagement further drawing the Federals toward the waiting main force of Confederates. As both sides fed more troops into the area, the battle escalated.

Just as the Federal line began to feel the demoralization of a fresh Confederate attack, a 30-pound Parrott railroad gun opened up on them. (A Parrott projectile will explode, send shrapnel in all directions, and cause a disastrous effect on infantry.) One of its heavy shells dropped in the middle of the 54th Massachusetts USCT with disastrous effects on its already weakened moral.

Seymour ordered a withdrawal of his army, and, as night fell, the Federal regiments were in full retreat, most of them in near panic and general confusion. Seymour made no effort to remove his dead and wounded from the battlefield, even leaving a wounded Federal battalion commander lying on the field.

The battle cost the Federal forces 1,861 killed, wounded, or captured. It was the highest percentages of Federal casualties recorded in any single day battle.

The Confederates captured large amounts of equipment, including five cannons and 1,600 rifles. Seymour had ordered 130,000 rounds of small arms ammunition dumped into a lake at Baldwin. The Confederates were able to salvage most of the ammunition.

The battle did little to advance either cause. The Confederacy had to commit troops to Florida that were needed for the defense of Savannah, Charleston, and Atlanta. The Federals accomplished none of its immediate goals. Within two days, the Federals were back in Jacksonville and under the protection of the warships in the St. Johns River.

Seymour reported that he had found no loyal sentiment whatsoever, and the idea of loyal sentiment in Florida was only a myth

# 9
## BATTLE OF CEDAR CREEK

*By Lydia Colee Filzen and used with permission.*

The Battle of Cedar Creek occurred March 1, 1864, in the aftermath of the Battle of Olustee, which occurred eleven days before. The Battle of Cedar Creek was the costliest battle in Duval County during the war, resulting in twenty-nine casualties.

After the Battle of Olustee, Confederate forces massed west of Jacksonville, which discouraged the Federals from venturing beyond their lines.

On the morning of March 1, part of the 2nd Florida Cavalry set out eastward toward Jacksonville on a reconnaissance to probe Federal defenses. That same day, an expedition of Federal cavalry left Camp Mooney and headed west on a reconnaissance to feel out the Confederate position. Their force, under the command of Major Stevens, consisted of Companies B, C, and D of the 1st Massachusetts Cavalry, a squadron of the Massachusetts mounted infantry, and one gun of Elders' Horse Artillery.

At mid-morning, the 2nd Florida stopped the Union advance about two miles west of Camp Finegan. The Confederates, now joined by infantry reinforcements, pushed the Union forces back through Camp Finegan. At Cedar Creek, six miles west of Jacksonville, the Union troops made a stand. The Confederates flanked the Union line forcing the Federals to retreat toward Three Mile Run.

The Confederates pursued and were ambushed by the Union rear guard. The 27th Georgia and 11th South Carolina crossed Cedar Creek and advanced toward Jacksonville. Meeting reinforcements from Camp Mooney, the retreating Federals were ordered to return to Cedar Creek.

Finding that the Confederate infantry had already crossed Cedar Creek in force, the Union troops retreated toward Three Mile Run and the protection of their breastworks. The skirmishing continued until dark.

During the battle, seven Confederates were killed and twelve were wounded. Union reports list two Union killed, three wounded, and five captured. Colonel Dickison of Company H of the 2nd Florida disputes the Union count, estimating that forty Union soldiers were actually wounded.

The battle at Cedar Creek convinced the Confederates that they could not retake Jacksonville. Southern forces remained in the area to guard against further Union advances.

# 10

## THE HILLSBOROUGH RAID AND THE
## BATTLE OF BALLAST POINT

A round the time of the start of the war, the Jean Street Shipyard was owned and funded in part by Tampa businessmen, James McKay and David Hope. McKay owned and operated a shipping line that ran from Tampa to Havana. He also owned the local salt works. He is credited with organizing the Cowboy Cavalry to supply beef to the Confederate armies. McKay, however, is probably best known for and perhaps immortalized for being a daring and brazen blockade runner.

Union gunboats controlled the waters of Tampa Bay from the naval base at Egmont Key and most of the Gulf of Mexico from the navy and army bases in Key West. But despite Federal efforts to cut Tampa off from the rest of the world, McKay and his fleet of blockade runners enabled Fort Brooke and the citizens of Tampa to export and import goods.

In 1861, McKay and his ship, the steamer *Salvor*, were captured by the Union Navy while returning to Tampa from Havana. The ship was carrying weapons and was seized. McKay and his son were arrested and imprisoned in New York. Within a few months, McKay's money, connections, and influence procured a personal pardon from Abraham Lincoln.

McKay and his son returned to Tampa. McKay believed that his ship, which was sailing under the British flag (as McKay was of Scottish origin), had been wrongfully seized and protested the seizure, as did the British government, but the Federal government refused to return McKay's ship.

One of the conditions of McKay's pardon was a promise not to return to the service of the Confederate cause, a promise the now bitter McKay abandoned. He armed one of his ships and attacked a fleet of small Union boats, which were not only supplying Florida fish to the Union, but also providing information about the positions of Confederate ships to the Federal garrison based at Key West. McKay captured over twenty vessels, earning a vendetta against him.

McKay returned to blockade running on his sailing sloop, the *Kate Dale*, and his prize vessel, a side-wheeler steamship, the *Scottish Chief*. According to Union records, it was the destruction of these two vessels and nothing more that was the actual focus of a massive attack against Tampa in October of 1843, dubbed the Hillsborough River Raid, which turned into the Battle of Ballast Point.

Tampa did not have much military significance, so the Jean Street Shipyard, located far up the Hillsborough River believed to be safe from Union attack. This did not prove to be the case in October 1863, the location of the shipyard and the *Kate Dale* and the *Scottish Chief* was made known to Admiral Theodorus Bailey of the Union blockade squadron. The two ships, along with the steamer *AB Nays*, were loaded with cargo and awaiting the signal to run the blockade.

Union forces shelled Tampa as a diversion to the actual mission, which was to destroy McKay's ships. The mission was aided in part by two Union sympathizers, Egmont Key refugees, Henry Crane and James Thompson, who had alerted the Federals to the presence of the blockade runners. The shelling, although only a diversion, devastated Tampa. Almost a dozen blockade runners operated out of the city, but McKay was the target, presumably for breaking the promise that freed him from Union captivity a few years earlier.

Thompson, familiar with Tampa and the Hillsborough River, led the hundred man Union expedition, fourteen miles by foot, to the Jean Street Shipyard. The expedition carried a small boat in case the soldiers needed to cross the river, but they hid the boat a few miles from their destination in order to speed their march. Somehow, the expedition ended up on the wrong bank of the river.

The surprised and equally disorganized sleeping crew of the *Scottish Chief* heard men calling for help from the other shore. Thinking the men were fellow crew, the men sent a boat from the ship. It was a ruse. The men calling for help were actually two Union officers and a hand full of the Union soldiers. The *Scottish Chief's* crew was ambushed, and the Federals burned McKay's boats.

McKay and two crewmen escaped, but five other crewmen were captured. The *Scottish Chief's* captain and two crewmen ran to Tampa and alerted the town and Fort Brooke of the attack. McKay stayed behind and watched as his ships were destroyed.

Another boat at the shipyard (name unknown) was also destroyed. The *AB Nays* escaped upriver, near to what is now Lowry Park, only to run aground and be burned by her crew to prevent the ship from capture. (Many Union ships were actually captured Confederate blockade runners, including the *Adela*, one of the ships used by the Union for this attack.)

Had the *Scottish Chief's* captain and crewmen not escaped, the Union expedition would have destroyed the ship yard. The expedition, now aware that the garrison at Fort Brooke would be alerted, and the primary mission now accomplished, quickly moved south toward their rendezvous point of Ballast Point, some fourteen miles away. The Jean Street Shipyard was spared from destruction.

Halfway down the river, some of the Union soldiers recovered the small boat they had hid and proceeded from that point by river toward Tampa. Along the way, some local militiamen, not very well organized and barely armed disguised themselves as Negro women and lured the Union soldiers in the boat to the bank of the river and killed or captured them.

The rest of the Union expedition proceeded by land to Ballast Point. Forty Confederate solders, under the command of Bragg, waited for them. Bragg just happened to be in Tampa as part of an expedition to protect a cattle drive that was leaving from Tampa to supply the Confederate front. A fierce and bloody battle ensued, which became known as the Battle of Ballast Point. Both sides incurred heavy casualties.

As often happened during the war, both sides declared victory, as both sides inflicted about equal losses and casualties to each other. In the Confederate record, the Confederate commander at Tampa declared that if he had had a few more men, he would have captured the Union boats as well.

In truth, Tampa suffered the most. The town was destroyed by the shelling, the residents were scattered, the blockade runners destroyed, and as part of the Union expedition, the McKay's salt works, near what is now the entry to the Courtney Campbell Causeway, was also destroyed. The destruction of the salt works was devastating to the people of Tampa, who used the salt to preserve their food.

Union Lieutenant Commander Alex Semmes, commander of the *Adela*, noted that he sincerely regretted the loss but felt a great degree of satisfaction in having impressed the rebels with the idea that blockade running vessels are not safe, even up the Hillsboro River. Blockade running, along with everything else, pretty much come to a stop in Tampa.

About six months after the attack on McKay's ships, the Union sent three more ships to Tampa and succeeded in capturing the city, destroying Fort Brooke and arresting more than forty of the eighty citizens who lived in the city. Union soldiers burned many of the remaining houses and buildings and looted what was left of the town, leaving the woman and children to fend for themselves. There was so little left of Tampa that all sides lost all interest in the city. Tampa sat mostly abandoned.

*Notes:* The remains of the *Kate Dale* are sunk near the west side of the shipyard. The *Scottish Chief* remained afloat after it burned and was towed back to Tampa by McKay, who stripped the ship of its fittings and furnishings and destroyed the rest. The remains of the *AB Nays* lies in the river just up from Lowry Park and can still be seen at low tide. Its sighting is often included in the Nature Boat Tour from Lowry Park Zoo.

# 11

## THE BROOKSVILLE RAID

*By Lydia Colee Filzen and used with permission.*

In July 1864, the Union sent four ships carrying troops and horses from Fort Myers north up the Gulf Coast to fertile Hernando County above Tampa Bay. The ships passed Anclote Key and unloaded near Bayport.

A force of 240 men from the 2nd Florida Cavalry (Union) and the 2nd US Colored Infantry disembarked from the ships. The Confederate home guard stationed nearby, seeing that they were seriously outnumbered and outgunned, fled inland and spread the alarm.

Some of the Union soldiers were natives of the area and familiar with the terrain. They raided their Secessionist neighbors, burning and plundering along a swath that was six miles wide. They confiscated foodstuffs, cotton, and livestock and took prisoners as they headed north along the path of the Anclote River toward Confederate-held Brooksville.

The Confederate home guard consisted of a few old men, boys, and members of the Cow Cavalry, who were regular army men assigned to the region to gather cattle and drive them to the railhead at Live Oak.

One of the cavalry man, Thomas Benton Ellis of Captain R.A. McKay's Co. C, 3rd Florida Infantry, gives an account of his part in the defense of Brooksville.

*Just as morning was breaking, I saw the Yanks coming; they were riding the captured horses. I sent Captain Delaney back at once, toward Brooksville, where a company of old men and boys were stationed, and told them to send a runner at once to Tampa and have Captain Leslie's company, and if possible, Captain McKay's detailed men to come at once. He left at full speed. I told him to send the old men and boy company at once, to come as far as a creek or branch about twenty miles from Brooksville and form themselves on this branch; that John Crighton and I would try to hold the Yanks in check as best we could till we could meet them.*

*We stayed just ahead of the Yanks, allowing them to get within speaking distance, and we recognized Pilto, a deserter and one of my neighbors. We kept our horses' heads facing them and moved backwards. They hollered at me and told me to stop, that they would not hurt me. You may be assured that I did not trust them.*

*We continued along in front of them for some miles until we reached the place I had ordered the Home Guard to form themselves. But as I got to the branch, I saw across on the other side, the men running all helter skelter, with no one and everyone in command.*

Despite the chaos, the defenders made a stand and the clash resulted in five Confederates wounded and three killed.

The Federals reversed course, plundering McKay's father's plantation along the way. Eventually, they retreated to their boats and steamed back to Fort Myers with their booty.

# 12

## BATTLE OF BOWLEGS CREEK

*By William Lloyd Harris and used with permission.*

War in Polk County? Not since the Indian Wars and the fight at the old Tillis Homestead would be the reply of most of the citizens in Polk County. Most are startled to hear that a clash between Blue and Gray actually occurred just south of Fort Meade. Though it doesn't figure prominently in the list of battles or cause historians to take special note, the events and deeds of that day form a colorful part of Florida's heritage.

Polk County was sparsely populated. Three years earlier there were just over 300 men registered to vote (not all were of military age) on this wilderness fringe of south Florida. At the onset of war, families, communities, and friends had been divided about secession. Union sympathizers, tagged as deserters to the South, abandoned their homes and trekked south to Fort Myers. Men loyal to the Confederacy seized the opportunity to serve – forming into military companies to prepare for war. Quite a number left the state as members of the South Florida Bulldogs (Co. E, 7th Florida Infantry) to fight in the Army of Tennessee. Still others did their duty on the battlefields of Virginia, and those left behind became soldiers at home.

South Florida was of vital importance to the Confederacy. The vast herds of Jacob Summerlin and a handful of other cattlemen roaming in the open range of the Peace-Kissimmee River Basin had become, by 1864, the sole meat ration for the Southern armies opposing Sherman in north Georgia. During the dry season, an average of 2,000 head of cattle per week was driven north. The cattle drive started at Fort Meade and wound its way through Bartow,

Brooksville, Gainesville, and then to Baldwin to be loaded on railroad cars.

In an effort to impede the drive and shorten the war, the Federals reactivated Fort Myers as an army post. They stationed five companies of regulars and rangers with orders to raid the herds and create turmoil where possible. In one year, these raids netted an estimated 4,500 head of cattle. The war in Florida rapidly became one for cattle. The Federals adopted a systematic strategy to steal or slaughter all the cattle possible.

It became necessary to find local men familiar with the area to help lead the raids. James D. Green had been an early settler (in 1851, Redding Blount purchased the Green home site, which consisted of much of present-day Bartow) and lived in and around Fort Meade.

A member of Captain William B. Hooker's company during the Seminole War, he roamed the Peace River Valley and became acquainted with the land and practically all the residents of this vast area. As a result, he applied for a commission in the Union army. He was said to have dash and daring for this peculiar kind of warfare, which is different from almost any other.

Now a first lieutenant, Green recruited thirty-four men, who mustered into the Union army as Company A, 1st Battalion of Florida Rangers. Later, after a regimental organization, the unit was known as Company A, 2nd Florida Cavalry, USA.

To provide some protection to the settlers and to guard the cattle drives, a unique, unconventional force of hard-riding cowboys, known as crackers, was organized across south Florida. The term cracker derived from the last twelve to eighteen inches of the whip used by the cowboys to herd and drive cattle.

Assigned to the Confederate Quartermaster Department, these men formed the 1st Florida Special Cavalry Battalion under the command of Colonel Charles Munnerlyn. Nicknamed the Cow Cavalry, they were a diverse group of veterans, old Indian fighters, ranchers, settlers, and Confederate soldiers. Most were local men, kept in communities where they could provide for their families. Some had been detailed from the battle front because of their knowledge in handling cattle.

Captain Francis Asbury Hendry's company of Independent Cavalry was stationed at Fort Meade. He and his men were primarily local pioneers. According to Munnerlyn's first official report, these troops were the most efficient of all. Their job was to guard against Federal incursions and head the cattle drive to its ultimate destination – the Army of Tennessee. They were so effective in driving off Union cattle rustlers that stealing in the area almost stopped.

Eager for a fight and, in conjunction with the larger strategy being played out in north Florida, Green led a Union raiding party up the Peace River Valley. He was ordered to capture horses and cattle and whatever supplies the settlers had that would be useful to the army. He also burned homes and buildings and destroyed crops. The homes belonged to men who were away fighting for the Confederacy. Their wives and children were left to manage as best they could.

The Federals rode approximately 100 miles toward Fort Meade to carry out their mission. The Confederates made their base of operations in a hammock[1] some four miles north of Fort Meade, near Camp Branch. Arriving in the Fort Meade area, the Federals raided the Underhill home, fought with local residents, killed seventy-five year old Jim Lanier, and traveled to the Willoughby Tillis home. Tillis was away at the time, and, as recounted by his son some years later, the Federals took all of the horses and wagons loaded with provisions, corn fodder, and meat, took the Negro men, and all firearms.

Green's official report stated:

---

[1]In the southeastern United States, a hammock is a stand of hardwood trees that form an island in contrast to the surrounding landscape.

> *...on the 13th and 14th, this company was engaged in skirmishing with guerrillas near Fort Meade and succeeded in driving them off and destroying all their stores. Killed one and wounded four others, captured twenty-two horses having one man slightly wounded.*

As a result of this encroachment, Confederate troops were needed in the area. Captain J.J. Dickison and his Company H, 2nd Florida Cavalry, operating around Palatka, was ordered to Fort Meade, only to be recalled to help counter the large Union movement from Jacksonville toward Tallahassee.

On the 20th, Green's detachment returned to the area. This time, the Federals were met by armed resistance, which Green estimated as 150 Confederates or more. Lieutenant F.C.M. Bogges, second in command of the Confederate Independent Cavalry, reported:

> *There were but few to meet and repel them. The settlers kept a scout on the road at all times (Benson's trail leading south to Fort Myers). When the Union troops came, the settlers would show their men first in one place and then in another. The Federals had long range guns and would shoot when they saw the scouts.*

Private Aaron E. Godwin of Hendry's Company pinpointed the fight as taking place at Bowlegs Creek.

The Federals inflicted yet another casualty during the melee. Thomas Underhill, a veteran Indian fighter and a participant in the Seminole War and the battle at the Tillis homestead, was captured and killed. Underhill and Green had been neighbors prior to the war. The Union cavalry crossed west over the Peace River, burned the Tillis homestead, and retreated to Fort Myers. They never raided that far north again.

Confederate authorities reacted sharply to this campaign of theft and slaughter. Major P.W. White, Chief Commissary of Florida, wrote General Patton Anderson and pointed out the value of Florida cattle to the Confederacy and requested immediate military action against the deserters. Anderson agreed to send troops as soon as possible.

Some months later, the 64th Georgia was sent to Fort Meade. Union forces refused open combat and moved from place to place in order to avoid contact, or they took refuge on the coastal islands where they were protected by the Federal blockading squadron.

At times, the reports of skirmishes or battles become exaggerated, and the true overall picture can only be seen by examining the records of both sides.

The Union force reported fighting 150 Confederate soldiers, while the Confederates reported that they met at least 1,000 soldiers. Green declared victory, yet at an awful cost. After the war, he died a very lonely man ostracized by his neighbors for the terror he had caused.

# 13
## BATTLE OF OLUSTEE

In early 1864, Lincoln actively supported plans to restore Florida to the Union. The three major objectives of the plan were (1) to cut off a very important source of supply for the Confederate Army, chiefly cattle, (2) to recruit slaves, both local and runaways, as soldiers, and (3) to implement the project begun in Jacksonville in 1862 to organize a loyal government. Lincoln was so encouraged by the optimism of a small element of Union people in the state that he gave his private secretary, John Hay, a commission as a major and authorized him to set up a loyal government. Lincoln believed the formation of the government would be largely routine once an expeditionary force landed in Jacksonville.

In February, 1864, the expeditionary force was sent from Charleston, under the immediate command of Brigadier General Truman Seymour. His total force numbered 12,000 men, infantry, cavalry, and artillery was to be used to occupy the state. The expedition was escorted by Union warships and, like two previous occupation forces, met with only token opposition.

Union regiments moved into the state along the Florida, Atlantic and Gulf Central Railroad, or along present U.S. 90. They met little opposition until their vanguard approached Lake City where Finegan had rallied 2,000 men to oppose them.

After a brush with the Confederates at Lake City, the Federals withdrew to Sanderson and established a base. Finegan followed to Olustee where he was joined by two brigades from Georgia sent by Beauregard. The approximate 5,000 Confederates partially fortified their position at Olustee and planned to meet the main Union Army there, but the development of the battle occurred three miles to the east.

## Preliminaries of the Battle, February 20, 1864

Finegan received a report that the Union Army was approaching Olustee from the east. He ordered Colonel Caraway Smith's Cavalry to advance. The 4th Georgia Cavalry, under the command of Colonel Clinch, advanced and dismounted as a skirmish line. The Georgians were supported by the 2nd Florida Cavalry. The skirmishers met the advance guard of the 7th Connecticut and firing began on both sides.

In keeping with Finegan's orders, the Confederate skirmishers fell back to draw the Union forces toward the main Confederate position. Meanwhile, the 64th Georgia, under command of Colonel George Harrison, took position behind the skirmishers and stopped the advance of the 7th Connecticut.

The 4th Georgia took position on the left flank of the Confederates and the 2nd Florida on the right flank as the firing became general. The 7th New Hampshire moved forward to the right of the 7th Connecticut with the 8th U.S. Regulars (USCT), a colored regiment, in reserve.

The firing became heavier. General Colquitt moved three of his Georgia regiments, the 6th, 19th, and 28th in support of the 64th. The 6th took a position on the left flank of the 64th and the 28th and the 19th were on the right. Captain Robert H. Gamble's Company, Florida Light Artillery unlimbered in support of Colquitt. Pressure from the Confederates firing caused the 7th Connecticut to withdraw. The 8th U.S. Regulars moved into position on the left of the Union line. The battle was now in full swing.

## The Main Battle

Seymour saw that the battle was now fully joined and proceeded to move his entire force into line of battle. The 7th New Hampshire deployed to the right of the Union line passing the 7th Connecticut who withdrew. The 7th New Hampshire also came under a withering fire from the Confederates. The regiment suffered heavy losses and was forced to withdraw. The 8th U.S. Regulars (USCT), moved into the right front of the Union line.

The 32nd Georgia moved into the Confederate line to the right of the 6th Georgia with the 1st Georgia to the right of the 6th, and the 23rd to the right of the 1st. These new regiments increased the fire power of the Confederate line.

The 8th U.S. suffered heavy losses. Its commanding officer, Colonel Frilby, was killed, his successor badly wounded, and command of the regiment devolved on a captain of one of its companies. The regiment was cut to pieces, lost its colors, and was in confusion and demoralized.

The flower of the Union Army, the New York brigade under the command of General Barton and consisting of the 47th, 48th, and 115th New York, was ordered into action. They were supported by the 1st U.S. Artillery with six guns, four of them twelve pound brass Napoleons, which unlimbered to the brigade's left and near Seymour's field headquarters. The Union front consisted of the 115th New York on the right, the 48th New York in the center, and the 47th New York on the left. Portions of the 7th Connecticut and the 8th U.S. had been partially reformed and were protecting the artillery on the left.

Gamble, supported by the Georgia Light Artillery, poured heavy fire into the Union line and received like response from the 1st U.S. Artillery. Because of a failure to receive necessary protection from its supporting infantry, the 1st U.S. Artillery was rendered ineffective, losing most of its horses and five guns, including three Napoleons.

Seymour ordered the remnant of the 7th Connecticut, the 54th Massachusetts (USCT), and the 1st North Carolina (USCT), of Montgomery's Brigade, to deploy through the New York brigade and take over the Union front line.

The Confederate front line had steadily moved forward until it had taken over the original Union front line. The 64th Georgia, under the command of Colonel Evans, and part of the 2nd Florida under Colonel Harrison, which had been in action and on the Confederate front line continuously since the battle began, ran out of ammunition. Other regiments found their ammunition running low. Frantic appeals were made for a new supply.

Staff officers, couriers, and orderlies rode back and forth between the Confederate ammunition train to the rear and brought cartridges forward in their haversacks, dispatch cases, forage caps, and anything else capable of transporting the desperately needed ammunition.

The 1st Florida the 27th Georgia and the 1st Georgia (Emmett Rifles), under the command of Captain A. Bonaud, moved forward through the Confederate front line to temporarily take over the front line until a supply of ammunition was brought up and distributed to the various Georgia units under Colquitt.

The presence of these new units had an encouraging effect on the Confederates. The artillery stepped up its firing. The Chatham Artillery, under the command of Captain Wheaton, replaced Gamble's Light Artillery and continued firing. When the battery began to run low on ammunition, Captain John M. Guerard's Light Artillery Company (Georgia) unlimbered for action. Colquitt ordered a section of the Georgia battery to support Wheaton. Guerard's guns brought a new supply of artillery ammunition.

The Confederate artillery joined the new infantry units in protecting its front lines during this ammunition crisis. This new impetus to the Confederate front caused General Barton of the New York brigade to send out an order for withdrawal.

Before the battle began, Finegan ordered Lieutenant Rambo of the Milton Battery of the Florida Artillery to mount a 30-pound Parrott rifle on a flat car and bring up a locomotive to move it. Rambo and thirteen men waited behind the Confederate line in a pine grove for a chance to use this railroad artillery. When the battle began, Rambo was afraid that firing the gun might cause trees and limbs to fall and injure Confederate soldiers. As the Union line was slowly pushed back, Rambo found that his gun could be advanced beyond the pines. Just as the Federals were suffering from a fresh Confederate attack and an increased artillery pressure, Rambo opened fire. One of the Parrot's heavy shells dropped in the middle of the 54th Massachusetts with disastrous results.

Seymour withdrew his army. As night fell, the Federals were in full retreat, some of them in near panic. Seymour left most of his killed and wounded on the field including Colonel Frilby.

### Epilogue – Retreat

Nearly all of the heavily depleted Union Army reached Barbers and Sanderson by midnight of the 20th, the day of the battle. The Confederates did not pursue.

Considering the number of men involved, the battle was one of the bloodiest battles of the war. Union losses were 203 killed, 1,152 wounded, and 506 missing. The Confederates suffered 93 killed, 847 wounded, and six missing. The Confederates captured large amounts of equipment including five cannons and 1,600 rifles.

In his haste, Seymour ordered 130,000 rounds of small arms ammunition dumped into a lake at Baldwin. The Confederates were able to salvage most of the balls or lead.

Within less than two days, the Union Army was back in the environs of Jacksonville and under the protection of the warships in the St. Johns River. There the army remained in a virtual state of siege for the next two months as the countryside was surrounded by Confederate troops who would repulse any patrols that attempted to leave the city. A lieutenant in the 54th Massachusetts wrote that Jacksonville, a pretty place, had been made lonely and desolate.

Seymour, reported to Major General Quincy A. Gilmore, Commanding Officer, U.S. Forces, Department of the South that he had found no loyal sentiment. The valor of the thousands who fought at Olustee, according to the prolific and popular American historian, Benson J. Lossing (1813-1891), proved that loyal sentiment in Florida was largely a myth.

# 14
## THE BATTLES OF GAINESVILLE

*By H. Reed Ellis and used with permission.*

T here were no guardian angels presiding over the Federal campaigns in Florida during the early months of 1864. Lincoln, misled by widespread reports of dissatisfaction among Floridians with the Confederate government, ordered General Seymour, who commanded the Union troops of the Florida District, to spearhead an attack upon Southern forces in the area so that loyal Floridians might be encouraged to rally 'round Old Glory once again.

As a part of this campaign, a raiding party of fifty men from the 14th Massachusetts Calvary, commanded by Captain G.E. Marshall, marched from Sanderson Station to Gainesville with orders to destroy any railroad cars in the vicinity. According to Federal reports, Marshall and his men arrived in Gainesville around noon on February 14 and immediately erected a breastwork of cotton bales to serve as protection against any unexpected Confederate attacks

This improvised fort formed a barricade around the town square and extended across four converging streets. That evening, the Union force was attacked by two companies of Confederate cavalry under the command of Dickison. The attack was easily repulsed by the Federals, who were stationed in a more favorable position behind their cotton enclosure. The Southerners retreated. The Federals occupied Gainesville for fifty-six hours before returning to Jacksonville on February 17. In accordance with previous instructions, no private property was molested or destroyed by the raiders, and the Federals even distributed Confederate stores among the needy inhabitants.

The colorful but somewhat different Confederate account is told by Lawrence Jackson and W.P. Settleworth, two Confederate privates who fought in the skirmish. According to their reports, Company C of the 2nd Florida Calvary, numbering from 100 to 150 men, under the command of Captain W.E. Chambers, engaged a Union force at Gainesville on February 15. The Confederates had camped in or near Gainesville the previous night enroute to Lake City to join Finegan's gathering army.

The next morning, after the men had received several bouquets of flowers from the town's patriotic ladies, the company marched from Gainesville. They were later overtaken in Newmansville by a courier from Gainesville, who reported that the Federals had arrived in the city just after Chambers' command had left. A vote was taken among the men, and it was decided to return to Gainesville in an effort to relieve the occupied community.

Chambers ordered a leisurely march back to town, and the command made several rest stops along the way. About four miles from their destination, Chambers' troops were joined by a few old men and boys, who were commanded by Colonel Louis Pyles of the 2nd Florida. Pyles had been wounded in Virginia and was home on leave from the Army of Northern Virginia.

The officers decided to enter Gainesville by way of two roads. Chambers and his men would enter through Cunningham Lane then up Liberty Street (now West University Avenue) and Pyle's small force would enter via West Main (now North Main Street).

When Chambers was near the Federal barricade, Lieutenant Samuel Reddick called for volunteers to follow him in a charge on the Federal breastworks. Twelve to fifteen men volunteered. They advanced in two columns towards the cotton bales. During the struggle, Sergeant Worrington was killed near the present corner of West University Avenue and N.W. 1st Street. Several horses were killed, and Reddick was seriously injured. The attack was repulsed, and the Confederates retreated to the Stewart place, eight miles west of town, where they spent the remainder of the night.

When Company C returned the next morning, they found that the Federals gone and had taken a large number of Negro slaves with them. Chambers pursued the invaders half way to Waldo before returning to Gainesville.

One Confederate, observing the fact that Pyles and his men failed even to make an appearance at the scene of the fight and witnessing Chambers' fear grow as the command came closer and closer to the Union enclosure, said, "The action was anything but credible to the officers in charge of the Confederate troops."

### Comments on the First Battle of Gainesville

As the reader will notice, there are a few incongruous statements which appear in these reports, and I would like to comment upon three of them.

If the Federals occupied Gainesville for fifty-six hours and arrived in Gainesville on noon of the 14th, as we are told in the official records, then it would only seem logical that the skirmish with the Confederates would occur on the evening of the 16th, and the Federals would have left about 8:00 p.m. that night. William Watson Davis in his book, *Civil War and Reconstruction in Florida* supports this view.

Of course there is the possibility that the battle was on the evening of the 14th, but this does not seem to be likely. If the above was true, then the Confederate force would have delayed their return for two days while the homes and businesses of their friends and loved ones remained in enemy hands, or the Federals would have occupied Gainesville for less than a day and would have spent two and one-half days and three nights wandering around the country side before arriving in Jacksonville on the 17th.

The Confederate account suggests that the battle was on the evening of the 15th of February, but if this were true then the Federals would have occupied Gainesville for less than thirty-two hours, or the Federals would have arrived on the 13th about noon. Both of the above possibilities are in conflict with the official records.

The second remark that needs clarification concerns the officer in command of the Confederate forces. The Federals firmly believe that they had defeated the intrepid J.J. Dickison and stated so in their report. However, as other facts show, the officer in command was Chambers. Dickison was, at the time of Chambers' departure from Palatka, somewhere along the St. Johns River on picket duty.

Finally, the Federal report stated that two companies of Confederate cavalry were engaged in the attack, but the facts show that only one company was engaged in the battle. However, there were two attacking rebel columns.

### The Second Battle of Gainesville

In August 1864, the seeds of conflict were sown again in Gainesville when a large Federal raiding party arrived in the city. The raiding party was under the command of Colonel Andrew Linturn Harris and was composed of men from the 75th Ohio, the 40th Massachusetts Volunteer Calvary, and the 3rd Rhode Island. This force was part of a general Federal offensive and was given the responsibility of occupying Gainesville, which, was at the time, a very valuable railroad depot for the Confederacy.

Harris marched from Baldwin on the morning of the 15th to Starke, and, the next day, resumed his march to Gainesville, which was reached on the morning of the 17th at about 6:00 a.m.

While the troops were eating breakfast, they were accosted, quite by accident, by a small force of old men and boys who were passing through town. This group, commanded by Thomas F. King, had no choice but to offer the enemy a fight. They were soon dislodged and sent retreating northward by the Federal force.

The Confederates were pursued by the Federals, who thought that they had defeated the evasive Dickison. After reaching the center of town, the raiders plundered and raided both public and private buildings.

Harris was informed by his pickets south of town that a large Confederate force was approaching. This time the Federals were the ones who were surprised. The men of the 40th Massachusetts were in the center of town with one piece of Federal artillery placed in their rear. The men of the 75th Ohio were near the railroad depot in the south of town, and there were other smaller groups scattered in other areas of the community.

At 7:00 a.m. the fighting opened. Dickison led the Confederates into battle near the depot. The 75th Ohio formed the right and left flank, both of which rested on a swamp near the depot, and the 40th Massachusetts was held in reserve. Dickison was held at bay, but the Southern troops surrounded the Union position via other roads. Harris' position became hopeless when his chief of artillery reported that the howitzer was almost out of ammunition, and his men reported that they had only a few more rounds left.

Having held the Confederates in check for two hours, Harris ordered a general retreat up the Waldo road. It was Harris' hope to rendezvous with Colonel W.H. Noble's colored troops, whom Harris believed to be between Magnolia and Starke. The last organized Union resistance was in front of the Beville House, and, from that point, the invaders were routed.

Captain Morton, leading the retreating Federal column with the howitzer, took the road to Newmansville. When Harris realized Morton's mistake, he pursued and overtook the column a few miles from Gainesville. Their combined force detoured around the town until they reached the road to Waldo, only to find Dickison's men waiting. In the battle, the artillery piece was captured. Harris and thirty-eight men retreated east until they reached the Bellamy road, which was about fifteen miles from Gainesville.

Harris predicted Confederate strength was from 600 to 800 men, while actually only 175 Confederates were engaged compared to the Union number of around 250 men. The Union defeat was complete. Total losses numbered 212 for the Federals, while the Confederates reported only two killed and three wounded. Reports later showed that this was an important Confederate victory for it secured South and Central Florida for the Confederacy for the remainder of the war.

## Comments on the Second Battle of Gainesville

It would be impossible to recognize the bravery of each deserving individual. However, I feel that I should call attention to two instances.

During the thickest part of the fight, much to the dismay of the men, the ladies of Gainesville ventured into the streets shouting encouragement to the Southern troops and repeating the orders of the officers. After the battle was over, these women administered aid to Union and Confederate soldiers alike and did everything in their power to soothe the pains of the battle.

During the Federal retreat, a small Confederate scouting party of four men captured a column of Union troops several times their size and brought the Federals to Gainesville to join the other 150 prisoners of war.

Finally, I would like to give a little more attention to Colonel Noble's march. Noble was ordered to advance to Lake City, but because of a misunderstanding, he raided the countryside above Gainesville and threw a severe scare into the inhabitants of the area. If Harris had been victorious, the way would have been clear for Noble and his colored troops to enter Gainesville and plunder the town.

# 15
## BATTLE OF MARIANNA

Marianna, Florida is a quite little town located seventy miles west of Tallahassee and home to Governor Milton. The town was established in 1823 and was named after Mary and Ann Beveridge, the youngest daughters of the original owner of the area. As county seat for Jackson County, Marianna was a trading post for the local farming community. The city was twenty miles from the Apalachicola River and the nearest railroad spur was at Quincy.

In 1861, most of the Panhandle remained isolated from the effects of the war. The Panhandle's main contribution was salt produced along the Gulf Coast. This area was also an important source of agricultural produce. Even though the area was sparsely inhabited, it heavily contributed soldiers to the Confederate armies.

In March 1864, Brigadier General Alexander Asboth, a Hungarian immigrant who was in command of the Federal Military District of West Florida, asked his chief in the Department of the Gulf, Brigadier-General Charles P. Stone, for permission to engage in active operations within the limits of his district. Although Stone said no, Asboth's enthusiasm was unquenched. In July, he proposed a raid on Columbus, Georgia, via Marianna and Montgomery.

In August 1864, Farragut's fleet forced a passage into Mobile Bay and the forts on the mouth of the Mobile and Tensaw rivers were captured. On September 12, 1864, acting on his own initiative, Asboth informed Stone that he would set out on a cavalry raid into the northeastern portion of West Florida with the objective of capturing Confederate forces in Washington and Jackson Counties.

On September 18, 1864, a mounted column of 700 union troops rode out from Fort Barrancas toward Jackson County. A small local Confederate cavalry was not able to stop Asboth's march.

As the Federal troops moved on, they spread out, destroying or confiscating local food and supplies. On September 23, the Federals also scattered a small, mixed company of militia/volunteer Confederate cavalry.

To disguise his intentions, Asboth sent a detachment to destroy Douglas' Ferry on the route that would take his expedition northwest of Marianna. On September 26th, his mounted troops skirmished with Captain Alexander Godwin's cavalry at Campbellton, only a few miles from Marianna. Asboth rested his weary men in preparation for a fight at Marianna the next day.

Campbellton was a crossroads, so the Federals could still move into Georgia or Alabama, or into the richest agricultural zone in Northwest Florida, or back southeast toward Marianna. Not knowing where the Federals were headed, Confederate Colonel Alexander Montgomery delayed gathering all his forces together and calling out the Marianna home guard. He attempted to picket the many crossroads with his small force, which prevented him from drawing his meager reserves together in a strong defense of any of the roads.

The Federals attacked Marianna at high noon from two directions. When Ashboth and the 2nd Marine Cavalry reached the LaFayette and Russ streets intersection, they were met by Montgomery and cavalry. The Confederates open fired and drove them back.

Asboth called out "For shame! For shame!" to his men as they retreated. The Federal troops regrouped and charged. This time it was the Confederates who retreated.

In anticipation of the attack, residents placed a wall of wagons, logs, and other debris across the street. The fleeing Confederates jumped over the barricades with the Federals in pursuit. Firing erupted, resulting in two things: First, the defenders at the barricade realized that they were in trouble and began to fall back. Second, the Federal troops continued to charge toward the barricade.

While Montgomery held off the Federal troops around the courthouse, the battle on LaFayette Street began to deteriorate. Most of the Confederate militia fled into the homes and buildings north of LaFayette Street, and the home guard slowly fell back to St. Luke's Episcopal Church.

Federal forces attacked with overwhelming force. Colonel Zulavsky ordered St. Luke's Episcopal Church burned with the Confederate wounded trapped inside. The burning of the St. Luke's Episcopal Church was the chief act of vandalism committed by the Union soldiers at Marianna. This occurred after the fight had practically ended, and the gallant home guard of old men and boys, well nigh defenseless, had paid the sacrifice. The church, which at the time was the largest and handsomest in town, was completely destroyed.

Most of the Confederate forces surrendered after severe hand-to-hand combat, but Montgomery led another force toward the river. Federal forces pursued and captured Montgomery at the courthouse. Approximately thirty of his men managed to escape and destroy the Chipola River Bridge before the Federals reached the river.

When the fighting ended, some ten Confederates lay dead or dying, sixteen were wounded, fifty-four men were captured. Thirteen of these were released. Among the wounded was dentist Thaddeus Hentz, who was the son of famed novelist, Caroline Lee Hentz. He was shot not far from his mother's grave.

Union casualties were eight killed or mortally wounded, nineteen wounded, and ten captured. Among the Federal wounded was General Asboth. His wound never healed properly, and he eventually died of from them in 1868.

Asboth decided not to head towards St. Andrews Bay. Instead, he headed to Choctawhatchee Bay. The Federals captured W.B.

Jones' scout company at Vernon, Florida, and sent them to Elmira Prison.

The memory of the spontaneous heroic and futile defense of Marianna on September 27, 1864, has long been remembered in Jackson County. A monument jointly erected in 1921 by the William Henry Milton UDC Chapter, the citizens of Marianna, and the Florida State Legislature memorized the battle with the following inscription:

*Battle of Marianna*
*September 27, 1864*
*Where Overwhelming Federal Forces were*
*Stubbornly Resisted By a Home Guard of*
*Old Men and Boys and a Few Sick and*
*Wounded Confederates on Furlough*
*1860-1865*
*Confederate Heroes*

# 16
## BATTLE OF NATURAL BRIDGE

The Battle of Natural Bridge was fought at what is now Woodville, Florida, just south of Tallahassee, on March 6, 1865. A small band of Confederate troops and volunteers, mostly composed of teenagers from the nearby school (which would later become Florida State University) and the elderly, protected by breastworks, prevented the Union Army from crossing the Natural Bridge on the St. Marks River. This action prevented the Federals from capturing Tallahassee.

Union Major General John Newton had undertaken a joint force expedition with the Navy to engage and destroy Confederate troops that had attacked Cedar Key and Fort Myers and were allegedly encamped somewhere around St. Marks. Due to shallow water and sand bars, the Navy had trouble getting ships up the St. Marks River. After finding one bridge destroyed, Newton decided to cross the river at Natural Bridge. The Federals started out before dawn and pushed the Confederate forces back but not away from the bridge.

Confederate forces under Brigadier General William Miller guarded all the approaches and the bridge itself. The action at Natural Bridge lasted most of the day, but after making three unsuccessful attacks, the Union troops retreated to the protection of their fleet.

### Confederate Account of the Battle

*The following account was taken from THE FLORIDA HISTORICAL QUARTERLY.*

According to the *Floridian* and *Journal of Tallahassee,* as copied in the *Florida Union,* news of the landing of the Federals at St. Marks lighthouse reached Tallahassee at 9:00 p.m. Saturday night (March 4, 1865).

The alarm was given, and the note of preparation sounded throughout the whole city and county and was extended to the other counties. The militia was ordered out, and a unanimous and invincible response was made to the call. Every man and boy capable of bearing arms was at his post. Never, since the first commencement of the war, have the people exhibited a greater spirit. One company of cavalry marched nearly sixty miles in twenty-four hours. Others marched on foot, thirty and forty miles to overtake their companies who had gone ahead, and, in a very short time, a sufficient force was on the way to the scene of action to meet any force the enemy had there.

Union General John Newton was to find that he was poking a nest of hornets.

In view of the scanty and incomplete muster records of the Confederate forces of Florida which have survived, and the meager references elsewhere of the units which responded to this emergency, it is impossible to list them in any degree of completeness.

It appears from Newton's report that he believed that General Sam Jones was mobilizing the available forces in Middle Florida. Jones made an appeal to Governor Brown of Georgia for aid, as Newton speaks of the arrival of 1,000 troops from Georgia. Jones did request that the rolling stock of the Savannah, Albany, and Gulf Railroad be connected to the Pensacola and Georgia Railroad via the newly reopened Lawton-Live Oak connection. It is more likely that Newton's information really referred to the arrival of the 2nd Florida Cavalry which, dismounted, arrived opportunely on the field at Natural Bridge and determined the outcome. They probably arrived from the east by train.

On the night of the 4th and morning of the 5th, in anticipation that an invading force might attempt crossing the bridge which spanned the river, a breastwork was thrown up.

Early on the 5th, Brigadier General William Miller went to Newport with a company of cadets from the West Florida Seminary and a small body of militia. This small force was steadily strengthened throughout the day. Federal troops, under the command of Major Edmund C. Weeks, on a reconnaissance expedition, and looking for an alternate means of advancing on Tallahassee, attempted to burn the Georgia Pensacola railroad trestle across the Aucilla River. Moving west toward Tallahassee, Weeks reached the primitive defenses at the St. Marks River and was repulsed by the small Confederate band. Assuming he was up against a much larger force, Weeks pulled back south toward the area around St. Marks.

With Newton's advance, Lieutenant Colonel Scott fell back with his detachment of the 5th Florida Cavalry battalion and two pieces of artillery to the East River Bridge. He removed the bridge's planking, unlimbered his guns, and prepared to offer some resistance. This stand could not be maintained long, as it was not desired to give the Federals occasion to discover a ford some distance above the bridge. Here, one of the cannon was lost. Four Federal dead were later found. Scott retreated to Newport, and, after crossing the bridge, damaged it sufficiently by fire to render it impassable. Buildings at Newport, including a foundry as well as a saw and grist mills were set ablaze in order to not obstruct the line of fire.

The reception Miller accorded Weeks lead Newton to conclude that passage of the river at that point was impracticable. Jones went to Newport on the night of the 5th. Miller, anticipating that Newton would make a night movement toward Natural Bridge, sent Scott with his cavalry to await them there.

During the night, Miller learned that the officer in charge of the small force left at the fort in St. Marks was alarmed by the advance of the Union fleet up the river and was preparing to blow up the magazine, burn the gunboat *Spray*, and put fire to some 600 bales of cotton at the port. Miller set off at once for St. Marks and arrived before the actions were consummated. His orders put an end to all thoughts of surrender of the fort. Miller returned to Newport before dawn and proceeded to Natural Bridge, which he reached an hour after sunrise.

Reinforcements continued to move throughout the night on the railroad. Jones ordered the troops to detrain at the turpentine-still at Woodville, a point closer to Natural Bridge than Newport. The plank road was thronged. The small force at Newport was ordered up, being later replaced there by Lieutenant Whitehead's section of artillery. This hastily assembled force of reserves, cavalrymen, and a section of artillery arrived at Natural Bridge a short time before 4:00 in the morning of the 6th. The entrenchment at that point had been thrown up earlier, in anticipation of such an emergency, just as the entrenchment at Newport had been.

On arrival, the troops were placed so as to extend the line, which originally was across the road, just in front of the bridge, so that the right and left flanks finally rested on the river below and above. On the left were Dunham's battery and the Gadsden Grays, with Colonel Love's militia in reserve near the left center. The West Florida Seminary cadets occupied the center, in front of the bridge. To the right was Scott's battalion of the 5th Florida Cavalry. Captain Houston's battery was to the left of the right center, to the right of which was stationed Colonel Daniel's regiment of reserves. The line thus formed a crescent, the concavity toward the bridge, which permitted a converging fire at the point where the Federal forces meant to cross.

Hardly had the line at Natural Bridge been formed before skirmishing began and continued until 10:00 or 11:00, during which period two attacks were repulsed. The fighting intensified subsequently, probably at the time of Townsend's advance, and continued heavily for three or four hours. Although each of the three Federal attempts to cross the bridge was made with marked spirit, they were repulsed each time with considerable loss. According to Jones, after the two initial attacks, the enemy formed under a cover of a thick hammock and kept up an obstinate fight at intervals for ten or twelve hours.

Early in the afternoon, Colonel Caraway Smith arrived with a battalion of the 2nd Florida Cavalry dismounted, which was placed so as to extend the line further down the west bank of the river. After a brisk fire from the four pieces of Confederate artillery, slackening of the Federal fire indicated their withdrawal. Thereupon Captain H.K. Simmons of the 2nd Florida was ordered to penetrate the hammock, and ascertain the position of the Federal forces. Observing felled trees and a breastwork, he, in disregard of caution, ordered a charge and was killed on the breastwork. This ended the fight.

The Federal retreat was covered by felling timber across the road, which had to be cleared before the Confederate cavalry could pass. Although pursuit was continued for twelve miles, removal of these obstacles so delayed the pursuers that Newton managed to withdraw without a rear guard action, and the Confederates returned to Newport.

When it was ascertained that the Federal force had re-embarked and withdrawn, the Confederate forces took up their line of march for Tallahassee on Thursday the 9th. On arrival in the capital city, they were addressed by Governor Milton in the hall of the House of Representatives, and, in complimentary orders by Jones, were allowed to retain their arms and equipment.

According to Jones, the Federal force landed at the lighthouse was estimated at between 1,500 and 2,000 men. Newton believed that he was opposed at Natural Bridge by a force likewise consisting of from 1,500 to 2,000 men. He stated that according to rumor, the Confederates were reinforced about noon by 1,000 veterans from Georgia. While no specific confirmation on this point has been encountered, it is surmised that if these troops may have actually arrived in Tallahassee but were detained to man the local fortifications.

It appears more likely that the report which came to Newton's ears of Confederate reinforcements arriving about noon, related to the arrival of Colonel Caraway Smith's men of the Second Florida Cavalry, who were indeed veterans. Newton also stated that he originally calculated on an available Confederate force of from 600 to 700 men, whose numbers through impressments might be increased to 1,000. That the Confederate position at Natural Bridge was well selected is confirmed by Newton, who stated that 200 resolute men, aided by artillery, could hold it against five times their number.

Newton declared that his expedition started from the lighthouse with 893 men, but detachments at Newport and at outposts up and down the river, together with losses in action, had reduced his force to 500 when the imagined Georgia reinforcements to the Confederates arrived. All Federal troops at Natural Bridge were from the 2nd and 95th U.S. Colored Infantry (the last described by the Confederate newspaper as the 19th Louisiana), with white officers.

It is doubtful if Jones had an accurate knowledge of the number of men who rallied to his call. Any estimate made at this date can only be a very rough approximation, based on the identifiable units in Soldiers of Florida. From this, the following data have been secured:

| Possible Unit | Company | Strength | Wounded | Killed | Notes |
|---|---|---|---|---|---|
| 5th | B,C | 97 | 1 | | Complete Roster |
| | D | 12 | | | Complete Roster |
| | F | 50 | | Treplett | |
| | G | 50 | 1 | Simmons | Mustered Out, April/May 1865 |
| Gamble | | 40 | 1 | | Mustered Out, April/May 1865 |

| Possible Unit | Company | Strength | Wounded | Killed | Notes |
|---|---|---|---|---|---|
| Dunham | Abell | 12 | 2 | | Mustered Out, April/May 1865 |
| | Dunham | 12 | 2 | | |
| Cadet | | | | | No Data |
| 1st | A | 17 | | | As Mustered Out |
| | B | 22 | 1 | | As Mustered Out |
| | C | 11 | 1 | | As Mustered Out |
| | E | 13 | 1 | Grubbs | |
| | F | 9 | 2 | | |
| | G | 7 | 1 | | |
| | I | 12 | 1 | | |
| 2nd Cavalry | A | 30 | 3 | | As Mustered Out |
| | I | 109 | 6 | | As Mustered Out |
| | K | 93 | 2 | * | As Mustered Out |
| **Total:** | | **595** | **23** | **3** | |

*Soldiers of Florida list 2 men named Henry K. Simmons as killed on March 4 (sic). One was listed as Captain Co. G, 5th Florida Cavalry Battalion, while the other was listed as Private Co. K., 2nd Florida Cavalry. They probably are the same individual who received a battlefield promotion and transfer.

This does not consider the unidentified units, the Gadsden Grays, Colonel Love's militia, or three other companies of the Gadsden County militia, all of whom may have comprised one unit. Their combined strength probably did not exceed 100 men. In the absence of data regarding the cadets, their number may be set at twenty-five.

Since the 2nd Florida Cavalry did not arrive until the later stages of the action, we may subtract their strength of 232 men from the total of 583 given, and add 125 as the approximate strength of the other units, for a total of 476, as an estimate of the strength of Jones' force for the greater part of the battle.

In round numbers, there may perhaps have been a total of from 600 to 700 Confederates engaged. What gives plausibility to this figure is the circumstance that all of the reported Confederate casualties, three killed and twenty-three wounded are included in the units for which figures are tabulated. Colonel Daniel was wounded by being dashed against a tree by his horse. It appears that the casualty figures relate solely to the action at Natural Bridge . It is not known what losses occurred elsewhere.

It would thus appear that there was actually no great disparity in the number of the contestants involved, and that each side grossly overestimated the number of its opponents.

Newton reported the following casualties, which probably cover the whole expedition, viz.:

| Unit | Killed Officers | Killed Men | Wounded Officers | Wounded Men | Missing Officers | Missing Men | Total |
|------|------|------|------|------|------|------|------|
| Staff | 1 | | 1 | | | | 2 |
| 2nd Florida | | 1 | | 2 | | 13 | 16 |
| 2nd US Colored | | 10 | 6 | 41 | | 1 | 58 |
| 66th US Colored | 1 | 8 | 2 | 37 | 1 | 23 | 72 |
| **Total** | **2** | **19** | **9** | **80** | **1** | **37** | **148** |

Newton stated that all of his wounded, except eight fatally wounded who were left at a house two miles from the field, were brought away. In some respects, the data of this table does not check with other information. Lieutenant Carrington (143rd New York) and Captain Tracy (2nd U.S. Co., A.A.A.G.) are the staff officers given respectively as killed and wounded. The name of the officer of the 95th US Colored killed is not given, but Lieutenant Colonel Pearsall of that regiment was wounded. Of the 2nd Regiment, Major Lincoln and Lieutenants Murphy and Seymour subsequently died from wounds, while Colonel Townsend was wounded but recovered. The Federal casualties were roughly sixteen percent of their force, or one for every six men. Assuming that the forces engaged were roughly equal in numbers, the Federal casualties were about seven times greater than those of the Confederates.

A few words may be said about the consequences of the sabotaging raids instigated by Weeks. Newton relates that the party for the Ocklocknee returned without making a serious attempt to reach the bridge. He complained that although the men sent were hand-picked, had good knowledge of the country, and could have, with little risk to themselves, obstructed the railroad for several days, so far as known neither of the bridges were damaged nor the railroad obstructed.

Newton however, either did not know or would not tell the whole story. The clipping from the *Floridian* and *Journal* in his hands contained a paragraph to the effect that on Tuesday last, (presumably March 7th) it was discovered that an attempt had been made to burn the Aucilla trestle on the Pensacola and Georgia Railroad. The damage was slight, insufficient to stop the trains, and the telegraph line was cut at the same point. This was supposed to be the work of deserters and may have been part of the program of the enemy to prevent troops from being brought from the east to take a hand in the late fight.

Strickland and one of his companions who were landed at the mouth of the Aucilla River were captured in Federal uniform with the aid of dogs, shortly after discovery of the fire at the railroad bridge. They were brought to Tallahassee, court-martialed, convicted, and shot on the 18th. Strickland had deserted from the Confederate service and became a leader of those in Taylor County disaffected with the Confederacy.

The Quincy newspaper also relates that two deserters were captured, summarily court-martialed, convicted, and shot on the spot. One surmises that the spot was Newport, and that the men were also from Weeks' command.

A great deal of hardship resulted in Wakulla County from the Confederate set conflagration at Newport. The same newspaper clipping previously cited relates that the loss of Mr. Dan Ladd's grist mill made corn meal scarce, and that destruction of the work-shops and sawmill was a great loss to the government, as nothing from either was saved. The bridge was easily repaired, as it had not been burned. Although Jones did not, in his report to General Johnston, cite any individual or unit for conspicuous service during the action, the Tallahassee and Quincy newspapers were generous in their praise, not overlooking any unit.

The reports available do not reveal just when Newton re-embarked his force at the lighthouse, but it does not appear that he tarried there. His earliest report on his subsequent activities is dated from Key West on the 15th, the day of his return. He later stated that after the expedition was over, the troops were distributed to the posts at Cedar Keys, Punta Rassa, and Key West, as Fort Myers was being reduced in troop complement.

Despite the whole-hearted spontaneity with which the people of Middle Florida rallied to repel the invasion, the success of their efforts could not change the worsening trend of events in areas beyond their horizon, nor postpone the inevitable. General Robert E. Lee surrendered on April 9, and General Joseph E. Johnston surrendered on the 26th. On the 8th of May, Admiral Cornelius Stribling reported to Secretary of the Navy Welles that the blockading officer at St. Marks reported that the authorities at Tallahassee are ready to surrender on the terms of Johnston's capitulation and were awaiting arrival of officers appointed by General Sherman. A few days later (May 10), Brigadier General Ed. M. McCook arrived in Tallahassee from Macon for this purpose, and received the surrender of 8,000 Confederate troops in Florida. Thus did Tallahassee, the only capital of a Confederate state east of the Mississippi River not captured by force of arms, render submission.

The opinion was entertained in Tallahassee at the time of the expedition, that Newton, on finding that his passage of the St. Marks River was blocked, might continue his flanking movement along the east bank, ascending to the head of the rise just south of the St. Augustine road near the Jefferson County line, and attempted to enter Tallahassee via the St. Augustine road. General Theodore Brevard relates that in anticipation of such a movement, the troops coming to reinforce the Confederates at the bridge were ordered placed in the forts around Tallahassee, especially in the fort on the hill commanding the St. Augustine road and the hill country to the east. This earthwork, well preserved, lies in Old Fort Park, Tallahassee.

Through one of those ironies of fate, the occurrence of which does not seem wholly devoid of malice, Newton, shortly after these events, did come to Tallahassee, and from the Headquarters of the District of Florida in that city, he himself issued General Orders No.1 on June 19, 1865, stating that in compliance with General Order No. 81, Department of the Gulf, he, as senior officer present, assumed command of the District of Florida, a post which he retained until the end of the following July. Major Edmund C. Weeks, during carpet-bagging days, is stated to have resided in Tallahassee.


NOTE: It does not appear that any issues of the *Floridian* and *Journal of Tallahassee* (a semi-weekly) for February and March, 1865 have survived. (See Elmer J. Emig: "A Check List of Extant Florida Newspapers, 1845-1876." *Florida Historical Quarterly* XI (Oct. 1932) pp. 77-87). One of Newton's reports is accompanied by an undated clipping from this newspaper.

# PART III

## Officers and Notable Leaders

# 17

## Brigadier General
## Theodore W. Brevard

Theodore Washington Brevard was born August 26, 1835, in Tuskegee, Alabama. He was a graduate of the United States Military Academy and studied law at the University of Virginia. He served in the Florida House of Representatives in 1858, and after the war, would serve in the Florida Senate from 1865 to 1866. He became the adjutant and inspector for the State of Florida in 1860, resigning this post at the beginning of hostilities to enter active service. He stated that he was too young a man to hold a safe and easy position while others were in peril.

He raised the 2nd Florida Regiment and after through training, the regiment became the first Florida regiment to be ordered to the state of Virginia. Brevard returned to Florida in 1862 to form a battalion of partisan rangers. Under the command of Brevard, now a lieutenant colonel, this battalion joined Finegan and was very effective in south and east Florida.

In a skirmish that occurred near Lake City on March 11, 1863, Brevard was commended for gallant conduct by Finegan, who, in a report of the skirmish wrote that his orders were executed by Brevard with promptness, gallantry, and discretion.

Following the Battle of Olustee, the battalion was ordered to Virginia with other Florida companies to join the 11th Florida under Brevard's command. Brevard was promoted to colonel. The regiment joined the Army of Northern Virginia on the eve of the battle at Cold Harbor. During the battle, the 11th Florida took part in the famous counterattack by the newly reconstituted Florida brigade that saved the day for the Army of Northern Virginia. Brevard was promoted to brigadier general and became adjutant to Major General George Washington Custis Lee. Brevard and most of the 11th Florida were captured at Sayler's Creek by General George Armstrong Custer in April 1865. Brevard had been a general for a little more than a week. It is unlikely that Custer knew he had captured a general officer, as he did not remark on this in his very detailed list of his achievements.

Brevard died June 20, 1882 and was buried in the St. John's Episcopal Church Cemetery in Tallahassee, Florida. Brevard County is named in his honor.

# 18

## BRIGADIER GENERAL ROBERT BULLOCK

Bullock was born in Greenville, North Carolina, on December 8, 1828, and moved to present day Ocala, Florida, in 1844, which, at that time, was a military installation – Fort King, named for Colonel William King of the 4th Florida Infantry and the first governor of the provisional West Florida Territory. The fort was built to protect northern Florida from the Seminole Indians to the south. Bullock taught in the first school in Sumter County and served as a clerk of the circuit court of Marion County from November 13, 1849 to November 11, 1855.

In 1856, Bullock was commissioned a captain by the Florida Governor and ordered to raise a mounted company of volunteers to defend the territory against the Seminoles. The company was mustered into service and served eighteen months until the cessation of hostilities.

In 1862, Bullock entered the Confederate Army as captain in the 7th Florida Infantry and served until the close of the war. He was promoted to lieutenant colonel in 1863 and to brigadier general in 1865. This promotion was backdated to November 29, 1864. Bullock took part in the Battle of Chickamauga, the Atlanta Campaign, and the Franklin-Nashville Campaign, where he was severely wounded.

After the war, Bullock studied law, was admitted to the bar in 1866, and began practice in Marion County. He served as judge of the probate court from 1866-1868 and was a member of the Florida House of Representatives in 1879. He was again clerk of the circuit court of Marion County from 1881 to 1889 before being elected as a Democrat to the 51st and 52nd Congresses (1889-1893). Bullock was not a candidate for re-nomination in 1892.

After leaving Congress, he engaged in agricultural pursuits. He was elected judge of Marion County in 1903 and served until his death in Ocala, Florida on July 27, 1905. He was buried in Evergreen Cemetery in Jacksonville.

# 19
## CAPTAIN J. J. DICKISON
## THE SWAMP FOX OF THE CONFEDERACY

With a very limited force, Captain John Jackson Dickison was largely responsible for keeping Florida from falling under Federal occupation.

Born in what is now Monroe County, West Virginia, he moved at an early age to South Carolina. Having prospered in business, he moved to Marion County, Florida in 1856 and settled near Orange Lake, a small community north of Ocala. He became one of the prominent planters of the area. Dickison had four children by two marriages. Two of his sons, Charles and R.I., served under their father in the Confederate Army. Charles was killed in action at Palatka on August 2, 1864.

From his later writings – and even some of his contemporary battle reports – Dickison seems to have been a rather pompous individual. This one minor frailty was more than offset by his personal courage and superb leadership ability.

When Florida seceded from the Union, Dickison began the formation of a cavalry company in Marion County. Before the organization was completed, John M. Martin, a leading citizen of the county, offered to join the company if it was converted to artillery. Dickison agreed with the provision that Martin become captain of the company while he served as first lieutenant.

While stationed near Jacksonville in May 1862, the Marion Light Artillery reorganized for the war. This necessitated another election of officers and, for some unknown reason, Dickison was defeated as first lieutenant. The blow was a severe one to both Dickison and Martin. At Dickison's request, Martin wrote to General Finegan, the district commander, requesting that Dickison be appointed as

119

quartermaster. Martin told Finegan that if Dickison was thrown out of the service, it would cause him much mortification and pecuniary loss.

Dickison was released from duty with the Marion Light Artillery on May 29, 1862. Although it had been a blow to his ego, his separation from the company led to his fame. Luckily, nothing more was heard about the requested appointment as quartermaster, and Dickison went back to his original plan of raising a cavalry company.

On July 2, Finegan authorized Dickison to raise the last company needed for the formation of the 2nd Florida Cavalry Regiment. The company, originally called the Leo Dragoons, was mustered into the Confederate service as Company H, 2nd Florida Cavalry, on August 21. Dickison became captain, William H. McCardell first lieutenant, and W.J. McEaddy second lieutenant.

Three days later, the company moved to Gainesville, where they remained a week procuring arms and equipment. Dickison's company was stationed in the Jacksonville area and skirmished with the enemy when the city fell on October 5. A few days later, the company was shifted about seventy miles up the St. Johns River to garrison Palatka.

From this time until the end of the war, Dickison was a constant thorn in the side of the Union Army and Navy. His company, along with various other units temporarily under his command, patrolled the areas along the St. Johns and eastward to the coast, ambushed Union foraging expeditions, and captured pickets and isolated bodies of troops. Even when he was not actually attacking the enemy, fear of Dickison and his men kept the Union forces bottled up in St. Augustine and a few scattered posts. The Federals could occupy the towns, but they were never able effectively to control the countryside. The Federals came to call Dickison Dixie and referred to the vast territory west of the St. Johns as Dixieland. It was during the last year of the war, however, that Dickison scored his most spectacular successes.

Dickison's command was ordered to the Tampa Bay area early in 1864 and had just arrived there when word was received of a major Federal advance from Jacksonville. After marching day and night for 575 miles to Tampa and back, Dickison's men were twelve hours too late to take part in the Battle of Olustee on February 20, which meant Dickison missed the one full-scale battle fought in Florida. His command managed to capture forty enemy stragglers as the beaten Federals retreated to Jacksonville.

On April 30, the Confederates learned that a Union force was at Fort Butler in Volusia County. Dickison was ordered to keep an eye on the Federals. He also learned that there was a Federal garrison at Welaka. At sundown, the next day, he moved with thirty-five men under Lieutenant McEaddy and Captain Henry A. Gray and twenty-five men of Company B, 2nd Florida Cavalry.

It was a nine-mile march to the St. Johns and, under cover of night, the men crossed in three small rowboats. Another seven miles brought them to Welaka. Placing two detachments on the flanks of the enemy, Dickison moved on the center with another detachment, capturing the pickets, and completely surprising the outpost. He demanded the post's surrender. The captain and a portion of Company B, 17th Connecticut, meekly laid down their guns. In all, the Confederates bagged thirty-nine prisoners without loss to themselves.

Dickison took his prisoners back across the river. After resting a few hours, he informed his men that he was immediately going after the Federal post at Fort Butler, about fifteen miles away and at the opposite end of Lake George. The entire command volunteered for the expedition, but Dickison took only twenty-five men. After some unfortunate events in the inky dark, the outpost, manned by a detachment of the 157th New York, was surprised and captured without resistance.

The capture of the two outposts caused consternation in the Union ranks. On the morning of May 21, Brigadier General George

H. Gordon, commanding the District of Florida, withdrew the troops opposite Volusia and Saunders on the river. Gordon started up the river by boat with 200 men of the Jacksonville garrison, accompanied by the gunboat *Ottawa* and the armed steam tug *Columbine*. At Picolata, he picked up six companies of the 35th United States Colored Troops and the remainder of the 157th New York, bringing his force up to about 650 or 700 men. The troops landed opposite Palatka and advanced overland while the *Columbine* proceeded up the river.

Dickison was in Palatka at the time, but he was unable to get a shot at the enemy across the mile wide river. When the *Columbine* started upstream, Dickison pursued along the shore with fifty of his men and two guns of Company A, Milton Light Artillery, under First Lieutenant Mortimer W. Bates. The Confederates arrived at Brown's Landing five minutes too late to engage the enemy. Dickison had gone ahead and concealed himself in a large cypress tree. The *Columbine* passed within fifty feet of him, and he had a good look at its armament.

Word then arrived from the troops left at Palatka that the *Ottawa* and one of the transports were coming upriver. Dickison halted his command about 300 yards from Brown's Landing. Bates unlimbered his guns. Dickison dismounted the cavalry and ordered them into the swamp to protect the artillery.

The *Ottawa* came upriver to support the *Columbine*. Gordon ordered the transport *Charles Houghton* to accompany the gunboat for protection. The gunboat anchored at Brown's Landing just as the sun set, and the transport dropped anchor astern. Lieutenant Commander S. Livingston Breese, captain of the *Ottawa*, not knowing why the transport was there, took the dinghy and went over to her. He had just boarded her when he heard the report of a field piece firing at the *Ottawa*. Breese jumped into the dinghy and was back on board the *Ottawa* before she had time to return the fire.

Dickison had placed Bates' guns in position when the two Union ships anchored. Just as the Confederates were ready to open fire, the enemy lit up their ships, making them fine targets. The two Confederate guns got off twenty-eight rounds before Breese was able to get his guns in action. Firing at the flashes of the Confederate guns, Breese believed he was being attacked by a battery of four.

Soon after the big 150-pounders of the gunboat opened fire, Dickison ordered Bates to withdraw his battery. The *Ottawa* had been hit thirty-seven times by grapeshot and had a shell smash through her smokestack, carrying away the mainstay. Breese slipped the anchor chain as soon as possible and continued firing long after the Confederates had disappeared. Neither side suffered any casualties.

The following day, May 23, Dickison selected sixteen sharpshooters and with artillery proceeded to Horse Landing, about six miles upstream from Brown's Landing. The guns were placed in position on the wharf while the horses and limbers were sent to the rear. The sharpshooters took their places behind cypress trees to the left of the guns.

The *Columbine*, acting Ensign Frank Sanborn commanding, was a converted steam tug armed with two 20-pounder Parrott rifles. Before she had left the landing opposite Palatka, sand bags had been piled on her deck to make her a little less vulnerable. A detachment of two officers and twenty-five men of the 35th United States Colored Troops under Captain Edward S. Daniels were on board.

In the evening, the *Columbine* returned downstream. Sanborn beat to quarters in expectation of an ambush. Upon turning the point just above Horse Landing, she opened fire on the landing and the road as soon as the guns could be brought to bear. She slowed down, and her torpedo catchers were lowered.

Dickison's men waited quietly as the Union boat drew nearer. When the *Columbine* was directly opposite the landing and less than 100 yards from shore, both of Bates' guns opened fire. Sanborn instantly gave orders to take up the battle, but Bates' second shot cut the wheel chains. At the same time, the pilot abandoned the wheel and jumped over the bow. The helpless vessel drifted about 200 yards away from the Confederate battery and 100 yards from the sharpshooters and ran aground on a mud bank. Another shell hit the main steam pipe causing a great loss of steam.

Sanborn left the hurricane deck and took charge of the forward gun, sending acting Master's Mate W.B. Spencer aft on the quarterdeck to ship the tiller and hook the relieving tackles, at the same time stopping and backing the engine.

Acting Third Assistant Engineer Henry J. Johnson now reported loss of steam, and Spencer reported that the quarterdeck had been swept by grapeshot and sharpshooters' bullets. The after gun had been abandoned and acting Master's Mate John Davis killed. Leaving the forward gun, Sanborn hurried to the quarterdeck. He quickly saw that the *Columbine* could not be moved. Their only hope was in driving off the Confederates.

Sanborn took charge of the forward gun and sent Spencer to rally the infantry guard, which was going over the side. Spencer managed to stop them, but Johnson reported that one of the after frame timbers had been shot away and locked the wheel, making the engine useless. Captain Daniels had been wounded, and the sharpshooters were picking off the men at the forward gun. Sanborn held a hurried conference with the surviving officers. They decided to surrender. The flag had been shot away at the beginning of the action, but Sanborn hoisted a white flag and went ashore to formally surrender his vessel to Dickison. The *Columbine* had lost one officer killed, five men wounded, and sixteen killed or missing. Apparently, several soldiers and sailors drowned attempting to escape. Because of the proximity of the *Ottawa*, Dickison quickly had as much property as possible removed and burned the *Columbine* to the waterline.

Dickison's next battle of the war came three months later. Early on the morning of August 15th, two Federal columns marched out of

Baldwin. Colonel William H. Noble had under his command three regiments of United States Colored Troops, twenty men of the 75th Ohio Mounted Infantry, and three guns of the 3rd Rhode Island Artillery. The other column, commanded by Colonel Andrew L. Harris of the 75th Ohio Mounted Infantry, consisted of the remainder of his regiment and one gun of the 3rd Rhode Island Artillery.

After following separate routes, the two columns met that evening at Trail Ridge. Harris soon resumed his march, adding to his column the twenty men of the 75th Ohio who had been with Noble. The column reached Starke at 2:30 a.m. on August 16th. Here, the column was joined by Captain Joseph Morton with two companies of the 4th Massachusetts Cavalry and a detachment of Unionist Floridians, totaling altogether 104 officers and men. The Federals camped at Starke until daylight and destroyed some Confederate commissary stores and railroad cars.

Dickison's company had been along the St. Johns, skirmishing occasionally with the enemy. On August 15th, they were at Waldo and soon found their communications cut by the advancing Federals. At sundown, Captain Samuel Rou with a detachment of his Company F, 2nd Florida Cavalry, arrived at Waldo and reported the enemy in Starke.

Harris resumed the march at 7:30 a.m. on August 16. His troops systematically looted the plantations along the way and rounded up the slaves. Dickison, learning that the enemy cavalry had left the infantry column behind, decided to give chase. To his own Company H, he added Rou's detachment, about twenty-five men of Company H, Florida Cavalry Battalion, a section of artillery under 2nd Lieutenant T.J. Bruton, and ninety new infantry recruits who had just reported. The Confederates moved out on the road to Gainesville.

Dickison left Colonel Elias Earle of Governor John Milton's staff in command of the infantry while he pushed ahead with the cavalry and the artillery. Early the next morning, Dickison was joined by a detachment of fifteen militia men, raising his total to 290 men.

After an all-night march, the Federal column reached the town of Rochelle at 6:30 a.m. on August 17. There were approximately seventy Confederate militia members in Gainesville, but Company B, 4th Massachusetts, easily drove them out of town.

Harris' horses badly needed rest and forage, so he ordered his men to keep on their accoutrements, but to slip the bridles and feed the animals. The cooks were ordered to make coffee. The 4th Massachusetts was near the center of town, the artillery piece to their rear, and the 75th Ohio to the rear of the artillery north of the railroad grade. The units were all in open lots, while mounted, and dismounted pickets were posted on all sides.

After driving into a small grove and feeding their horses, the Rhode Island Artillerymen took a walk through the town. Some obtained corn cakes, some a little rock candy, and some managed to secure Confederate money for souvenirs. They had just returned to the grove and were preparing to relax when a solid shot crashed over their heads.

Two miles out of Gainesville, Dickison sighted the enemy's rear guard. A mile closer, he ran into the Federal picket line. Dickison ordered Bruton to fire two shells into the enemy. Besides breaking up the Rhode Islanders' siesta, this fire hurried the Federals into position. Harris immediately ordered his command to face to their former rear, throwing the right flank of the 75th Ohio to the left to rest on a swamp and a thicket, and the left flank to the right, also covered by a swamp and a thicket. The howitzer was placed near the road, close to the center of the line. The 75th Ohio was dismounted, except for Company I, which was sent to guard the north side of town. The Ohioans took cover behind the railroad fill and neighboring fences. The 4th Massachusetts was held in reserve.

After driving in the pickets, Dickison dismounted his men, except for a platoon under McEaddy. He ordered Rou and McCardell to take the railroad depot, while McEaddy was to attack on the right, while 1st Lieutenant A.J. Dozier of the 5th Florida Cavalry Battalion drove the enemy from what is now University Avenue. Bruton's guns kept up a hot fire on the enemy.

The Federals were driven from the depot. The Confederates managed to lay down a crossfire on the enemy gun, cut down five of the six horses on the caisson, and kill the soldier holding the horses. The Rhode Islanders fired furiously, soon getting the range of Bruton's guns. Bruton told his gunners that this is no place to fight. Limber up! He moved his guns and quickly began to make it hot for the Rhode Islanders.

The Confederates began to close a ring around the town. Harris ordered Company B, 4th Massachusetts, to the rear of the town and threw out portions of the 75th Ohio farther on the right and left flanks. Harris decided his only hope was to cut his way out and try to find Noble's column, which was somewhere between Starke and Magnolia.

The Confederates were right behind the Federals as they left the firing line, leaving Harris no time to form his men into a column. By mistake, Captain Morton led a portion of the command out the Newnansville Road that went to the northwest toward Alachua instead of northeast on the Waldo Road, thus giving a large separation of the two elements. Private George H. Luther of the artillery detachment later recalled that they were in doubt which way to turn when the retreat was ordered.

After entering the Newnansville Road, Morton turned down a cart path, hoping to pass around and regain the road by which they had entered town. The Confederates were right behind them. Luther did not even stop for a large log across his path. The bounce over the log threw off some of the men astride the gun. One of the wheel horses was hit, and the gun came to a stop.

As soon as Harris realized that Morton had taken the wrong road, he dashed after him. By making a detour around the town, Harris brought a portion of the command back to the Waldo Road. About a mile from town, Luther came up with the disabled gun.

As Luther put it: "Colonel Harris, who was near us at the time, said: 'Boys, I am sorry for you; I have stayed by you till the last minute; good bye'; and away he went through the dust on his splendid horse." The Confederates closed in and captured the Rhode Islanders.

Dickison hurried through the streets as the Federals pulled out, calling to his men to mount their horses and give chase. Part of the enemy was pursued fifteen miles to Newnansville. Morton and most of his men were captured. Harris, three officers and thirty-eight men, abandoned the gun and its crew, turned off the Waldo Road, and struck overland for the St. Johns, reaching safety at Magnolia. The remainder of the command appears to have scattered.

Only 175 men of the Confederate force were actually in the battle. The remainder did not come up until after the fight was over, but they scoured the country for more than forty miles from Gainesville. Enemy stragglers were picked up for the next several days.

Major George B. Fox of the 75th Ohio and two of his men left town on foot, their horses having been killed, and were captured when they had almost reached the St. Johns River, fifty miles from Gainesville. Fox was brought to Dickison who pleasantly asked, "Major Fox, how is it that you allow the Gray Fox to outrun and capture the Red Fox?"

The advance of the main retreating Federal column, commanded by Lieutenant Colonel Benjamin Morgan of the 75th Ohio, was forced off the Waldo Road by the Confederates and took the Lake City Road. They struck east and eventually reached Magnolia. Morgan was captured in the swamps after his horse became disabled.

Harris had about 300 men in the battle. He admitted a loss of 176, but Confederate accounts state that twenty-eight were killed, five wounded, and 188 captured. In addition, Dickison secured the 12-pounder howitzer, 260 horses, and three supply wagons, as well as recovering about 200 slaves and the valuables looted from the plantations. The Confederates lost three killed and five wounded two of them mortally.

Although Gainesville was by far Dickison's greatest victory, he scored several more spectacular successes before the end of the war. In October, he ambushed the 4th Massachusetts, which was on a cattle raid, killing ten or twelve and taking twenty-three prisoners without any loss to his command. In February 1865, he attacked an expedition of the 17th Connecticut Infantry, which was seizing cotton near Lake George. In a sharp skirmish, the Confederates killed four Federals, including the regimental adjutant, and captured fifty-one soldiers, eighteen Confederate deserters and Unionists, and ten wagons full of cotton.

In a hand-to-hand encounter on horseback Dickison mortally wounded and captured Lieutenant Colonel Albert H. Wilcoxson of the 17th Connecticut, the commander of the expedition.

Immediately after his return, Dickison was ordered to the other side of the peninsula where a raiding party had penetrated the interior from Cedar Key. In a sharp engagement on February 13, the Confederates hotly pressed the 2nd United States Colored Troops and the 2nd Florida Cavalry (Union) until their ammunition ran out. The Federals lost six killed, eighteen wounded, and three captured while Dickison had five men wounded.

The end of the war found Dickison and his men again stationed at Waldo. Dickison surrendered and was paroled on May 20, still a captain despite repeated efforts by his commanders to get him a promotion. A few days later, Secretary of War John C. Breckinridge, fleeing the country after the collapse of the Confederacy, arrived in Gainesville carrying Dickison's appointment as colonel, which had been made on April 6.

The achievements of Dickison and his men are amazing when one considers the extent of territory in which he operated, the disparity in the size of the opposing forces, and the difficulty of the terrain. At one time or another, Dickison's command served from

Cedar Key on the Gulf of Mexico to Smyrna on the Atlantic and from Tampa Bay to Olustee near the Georgia border. He seldom commanded over 200 men at one time and never had more than two pieces of artillery, and these only during the last year of the war. But he inspired such terror in the Federal forces that even a rumor of his being in the field caused consternation. Federal commanders were constantly reporting that he had crossed the St. Johns with 100 men, while he seldom actually operated east of the river with more than fifty men. The Federal accounts of the Battle of Gainesville put the Confederate force as high as 1,000 men.

Although his military training had been limited to a brief time in the pre-war South Carolina militia and the first year of the war with the Marion Artillery, Dickison seems to have been one of those rare, natural-born soldiers. He skillfully used the swamps, the pine forests, the palmetto scrub, and the thick cypress trees to screen his small force. Repeatedly, he was able to place his men in positions from which they could ambush larger Federal forces. His ability to drive home a surprise attack is evidenced by the comparatively light casualties suffered by his command. His men idolized him, and he became the greatest hero of the war to Floridians.

In 1864, the Florida Legislature voted Dickison and his command their thanks. Major General Sam Jones, Brigadier Generals Joseph Finegan and John K. Jackson, Dickison's commanders, repeatedly commended him and urged his promotion.

Almost unknown today outside of Florida, Dickison was one of the ablest guerrilla commanders produced not only during the War Between the States, but probably in all American military history. To him must go most of the credit for keeping Florida as Confederate territory to the end of the war. Dickison must also be credited with maintaining a well-disciplined military unit. Even though operating often as irregulars behind the enemy lines, his men never committed the excesses often perpetrated by guerrillas on both sides of the war.

## Northeast Florida During the Civil War

GA
FLA

Oustee

Baldwin

Barber's (MacClenny)

Starke

Santa Fe River

Waldo

New River

Middleburg

Black Creek

Gainesville

Ocala

Orange Creek

Orange Springs

St. Mary's River

Kings Ferry

GA

Ft. Clinch

Fernandina Beach

Callahan

Trout River

Jacksonville

Mandarin

St. Johns River

Picolota

St. Augustine

Deep Creek

Palatka

Oklawaha River

Welaka

Ft. Gates

Lake George

Ft. Butler

Volusia

Mayport

Atlantic Ocean

Haw Creek

**The Campaigns of J.J. Dickison**

# 20

## BRIGADIER GENERAL JOSEPH P. FINEGAN

By William D. Hogan, Jr., Past Commander, Colonel L.M. Park, MOSB
Chapter 52.

*"Finegan, me bye, you know ye are yur mither's darling."*

Thus it is recorded as just one example of the colorful dialect of this native Irishman, born November 17, 1814, at Clones, Ireland. Like thousands of other sons of Eire, Joseph Finegan immigrated to the United States in the 1830s, settling in Florida near Rutledge where he became a prominent member of the community, operating first a small plantation and later a sawmill. A few years later, he moved to Fernandina and began a long association with the influential politician, David Yulee. Together they began construction of a railroad, and Finegan's importance rose in tandem with Yulee's.

Finegan was a member of the Florida Secession Convention. Without prior military service or training, until he entered the Confederate service, Finegan supervised Florida's military affairs under Governor Milton.

The political necessities of appointing a sufficient number of brigadier generals from Florida induced President Jefferson Davis to tender Finegan a commission on April 5, 1862. The Senate confirmed the appointment the same day, and Finegan accepted it on April 17, 1862. He became one of the senior officers appointed from Florida. He served throughout the war as a brigadier general.

Finegan took command of the Department of Middle and Eastern Florida, which he held for the next two years. It was a backwater command, important for protecting the long coastline and recruiting troops, often for service elsewhere.

Soon after Finegan took command, General Robert E. Lee complimented him on his zeal and productivity in organizing the Floridians into companies. Lee was also encouraged by Finegan's realistic attitude that only as many state troops should be kept in Florida as needed, while the majority should go to the main army of Virginia. Lee felt that he could not remove Finegan from Florida.

Finegan began to participate in action against Federal amphibian raids along the coastlines as the Union Navy tried to consolidate their position. While keeping his headquarters at Tallahassee, he commanded the defense of Tampa during the summer. In September, 1862, he took and occupied St. John's Bluff. Six months later, he captured Jacksonville and held the city briefly. He also distinguished himself and his Florida troops at the Battle of Olustee.

In May, 1864, Lee requested that the Florida brigade serving in the Army of Northern Virginia be enlarged and commanded by General Finegan. The Florida brigade fought at Cold Harbor, plugged the gap in the line, and won commendations from many quarters. Finegan's brigade was assigned to Mahone's division of the Third Corps. Throughout the remaining months of 1864, Finegan led the 2nd, 5th, 8th, 9th, 10th, and 11th Florida in the trenches of Petersburg.

In January 1865, prominent Floridians petitioned the Confederate government to have Finegan returned to Florida. On March 20, 1865, he was reassigned to overall command in Florida. In May, he rendered his final services to the Confederate States of America by aiding Secretary of War John C. Breckinridge's and Secretary of State Judah P. Benjamin's escapes through Florida to Cuba and the Bahama Islands respectively

After the war, Finegan lived in Jacksonville and Rutledge and worked as a cotton broker and practiced law. He served a term in the Florida Senate (1865-1866). He also employed his commercial talents in the cotton trade in North Florida and Savannah, Georgia.

He died on October 29, 1885, in Rutledge and is buried in the Old City Cemetery in Jacksonville.

# 21

## BRIGADIER GENERAL JESSE JOHNSON FINLEY

T he son of a wealthy planter, Jesse Johnson Finley was born in Wilson County, Tennessee, on November 18, 1812. He was educated at an academy in Lebanon, Tennessee before reading law in Nashville. After being admitted to the bar, he opened a law office in Lebanon. During the 1836 Seminole War, Finley organized a company of mounted volunteers and was appointed captain. He served in Florida for two years.

Moving often over the next few years, Finley continued to practice law and became active in politics. In 1841, he was elected state senator from Mississippi County, Arkansas. He resigned his seat in 1842 and moved to Memphis, Tennessee.

Finley was elected mayor in 1845, but in 1846, moved to Marianna, Florida. He was elected a Florida state senator in 1850 and in 1852, served as a Whig presidential elector. From 1853 to 1861, he served as a judge for Florida's western circuit.

After Florida seceded in 1861, Finley became a Confederate district judge. He resigned in March 1862 to enlist as a private in the 6th Florida Infantry. Probably because of his political prominence, Finley quickly rose to captain and then to colonel of the regiment. Attached to Colonel W.G.M. Davis' Florida brigade in eastern Tennessee, the regiment invaded Kentucky with Florida General Edmond Kirby-Smith's column during the late summer of 1862. Following the invasion, Finley oversaw the East Tennessee Department's court-martial court at Knoxville, Tennessee.

Finley's first real combat experience came at Chickamauga, where the 6th Florida was in Colonel Robert C. Trigg's brigade. On the afternoon of September 19, 1863, the Florida brigade was ordered to support an attack by John Bell Hood. The order to advance somehow miscarried, and Finley soon found himself several hundred yards ahead of the rest of the brigade. Nonetheless, the 6th Florida broke through one Union line and captured a battery of artillery. The markers on the field tell much of what the Floridians did. No other brigade won more honors at Chickamauga. The regiment suffered heavy casualties but earned praise from their superiors. After suffering the loss of 165 men, Finley was forced to withdraw.

Trigg wrote of Finley's command that the fortune of war threw the 6th Florida Regiment into the post of danger and upon them fell the heaviest loss and proved them veterans in their first fight. The next day, Finley drew praise when he led the 6th Florida and 54th Virginia in a charge against a Union position and captured 500 prisoners.

On November 8, 1863, Finley was promoted to brigadier general, to rank from November 16, and given command of the Florida infantry in the Army of Tennessee. He apparently was taken aback by the promotion and wrote Jefferson Davis to assure the president he did not seek the rank. On December 16, Davis wrote:

> *The fact that you did not seek the appointment conferred upon you, and your diffidence in assuming its responsibilities, is to me additional evidence of your fitness to command. I shall but the more confidently rely on one who, ready to serve, does not aspire to command.*

Finley's new brigade was placed in line with the Army of Tennessee near Chattanooga. When the Federals broke through the Confederate line at Missionary Ridge on November 25, 1863, Finley's brigade performed admirably in rear guard action, giving the army the time to escape. Bragg said, "I cannot, in justice to the generous and brave, consistently close this without expressing my thanks to

Brigadier General Finley for his gallant bearing and prompt assistance in every emergency."

The winter was a severe hardship for Finley's men. In February 1864, the officers of the Florida brigade forwarded a petition to Finley to be sent to Congress. The officers attached a list showing the outrageous prices they were forced to pay for food and clothing and declared they could not survive on the meager pay allotted them. Finley supported his officers, endorsed the petition, and forwarded it to his superiors, but apparently Congress took no action on the petition by Congress.

During the Atlanta Campaign, Finley's brigade was in Bate's division of William Hardee's corps. Finley saw heavy fighting in the campaign, but there is little official documentation of it. At Resaca, he was badly wounded and put out of action until the army reached Atlanta. At Jonesboro, shell fragments killed his horse and severely wounded him, but he refused to be evacuated to Atlanta until all of his wounded men had been removed. Because of this sense of duty, he missed the last evacuation train. He was laid in a wagon and was forced to slip through roving bands of Federals to reach the hospital.

Finley was separated from his brigade for the rest of the war. After recovering his wounds, he tried to rejoin his unit in North Carolina, but Federal troops blocked his way. He therefore reported for duty to Howell Cobb at Columbus, Georgia, and surrendered there in April 1865.

After the war, Finley settled in Lake City, Florida, and resumed his law practice. He moved to Jacksonville in the 1870s. Finley reentered politics and served in Congress from 1875 to 1879 before losing his seat in 1879 in a contested election.

In 1887, he was appointed to the United States Senate to fill a vacancy but was refused the seat because of a technicality. Returning to the legal profession, Finley served as a Florida circuit court judge from 1887 to 1903. He died in Lake City on November 6, 1904, and is buried in Gainesville.

# 22

## MAJOR GENERAL WILLIAM W. LORING

orn in Wilmington, North Carolina, on December 4, 1818, Loring was a direct descendant of John and Priscilla Alden of Plymouth Colony. At the age of five, his family moved to St. Augustine in the new territory of Florida. Little is known of Loring's early life beyond his family having a certain wealth. The family owned a mansion and an orange plantation. One account describes him as a handsome child, with fine earnest eyes, waving hair, and fearless spirit.

At fourteen, Loring volunteered for the Florida Militia. As part of the 11th Regiment, 2nd Brigade, he fought in the escalating skirmishes between the settlers and the Seminole Indians. In December 1835, the conflict erupted into war. On New Year's Eve, Loring took part in the Battle of Withlacoochee.

After a lengthy siege, Mexican General Antonio López de Santa Ana and his army of 4,000 defeated fewer than 200 Texans at the Alamo. News of this heroic defense spread rapidly across the country, and soon men were headed to Texas to avenge death of Davy Crockett and William Travis. Loring was seventeen when he ran away to join the War for Texas Independence. Loring's adventure did not last long as his father Reuben Loring arrived to collect his son and return home to Florida.

During the Second Seminole War, Loring fought at Wahoo Swamp and Alachus. At seventeen, he quickly distinguished himself and was promoted to sergeant and to second lieutenant at eighteen. Loring was now an officer and was beginning a military career that would last for more than fifty years and service on at least three continents. By 1837, the Seminole War was winding down and Loring was sent to the Alexandria Boarding School in Virginia where he completed his preparatory school before briefly attending Georgetown College (now Georgetown University).

Returning to Florida, Loring worked for Yulee as a law clerk. During this time, Loring completed his studies and was admitted to the bar in 1845. He began to practice law in St. Augustine and served in the Florida House of Representatives from 1843 to 1845, the year Florida was admitted as a state. He made an unsuccessful bid for the Florida Senate.

In May of 1846, Congress authorized the formation of a Regiment of Mounted Riflemen. Loring left his practice and joined the United States Army. This unit was originally organized to protect the Oregon Territory, but the regiment was sent to fight against Mexico. Captain Loring was quickly promoted to regimental major. On March 9, 1847, the Rifles waded ashore near Vera Cruz, one of the first to go ashore. While leading the charge into Mexico City, his arm was shattered by a bullet. The arm would later have to be amputated. Loring was brevetted to lieutenant colonel and finally to colonel.

Upon his return from Mexico, Loring was put in charge of the Oregon Territory. He led a train of 600 mule teams 2,500 miles from Missouri to Oregon. He commanded the Oregon Territory for two years. He was then assigned to command the frontier forts and engaged in numerous skirmishes with Indians. In December 1856, at the age of thirty-eight, he was promoted to colonel, the youngest in the army.

Loring left the army and traveled Europe to study the military tactics that had been invented during the Crimean War. Before returning home, he visited many European countries.

When the war began, Loring was in New Mexico. He decided to defend his homeland. He told his officers that since the South was his home, he was going to throw up his commission, and join the Southern Army, and each of you can do as you think best. He resigned from the Army on May 13, 1861.

Loring became one of the more troublesome of Confederate generals, frequently engaged in disputes with his superiors. His Confederate assignments included:

* 1861 – (May 20) Promoted to brigadier general.
* 1861 – (July 20 – August 3) Commanded Army of the Northwest.
* 1861 – (August 3) Demoted to brigade command in the Army of the Northwest.
* 1861 – (October) Commanded brigade in the Army of the Northwest.
* 1862 – (February 17) Promoted to major general.
* 1862 – (May 8) – Given command of Department of Southwestern Virginia.
* 1863 – Division commander of the 2nd Military District, Department of Mississippi and East Louisiana.
* 1863 – (April) Division commander, Department of Mississippi and East Louisiana.
* 1863 – (May 16) Division commander, Department of the West.
* 1863 (July) Division commander, Department of Mississippi and East Louisiana.
* 1864 (January 28) Division commander, Department of Alabama, Mississippi, and East Louisiana.
* 1864 (May) Transferred to the Army of Mississippi.

While serving under Robert E. Lee in the first summer of the war, he took part in the disappointments of the campaign in western Virginia. That winter, his command was placed under the overall command of Stonewall Jackson. Following the Romney Campaign, Loring opposed the stationing of his men in the exposed town and obtained orders from Secretary of War Judah P. Benjamin to move to

Winchester. Outraged, Jackson threatened to resign and was eventually upheld in his views of military etiquette.

On February 9, 1862, Loring was removed from his post, but a few days later was appeased with promotion to major general. After departmental command in Southwestern Virginia, he was named to command a division in Mississippi.

Frequently in conflict with department commander John C. Pemberton, he fought in the Vicksburg Campaign until cut off from the rest of Pemberton's force at Champion Hill. The two generals blamed each other for the defeat. Loring joined the forces under Joseph E. Johnston and took part in the defense of Jackson, Mississippi, and the Meridian Campaign.

By now he was known to his men as "Old Blizzards" because of his battle cry "Give them blizzards, boys!" Transferred to Georgia, he fought in the Atlanta Campaign.

When Leonidas Polk was killed at Pine Mountain, Loring briefly took charge of the corps, but was succeeded the same day by Alexander P. Stewart. Loring was wounded at Ezra Church and was out of action until after the fall of Atlanta. He then fought at Franklin, Nashville, and in the Carolinas.

From 1869 to 1879, he joined about fifty Confederate and Federal Veterans and served in the army of Isam'il Pasha, the Khedive of Egypt. Loring was a division commander in Egypt and upon his return was called Pasha Loring.

# 23

## STEPHEN MALLORY
## THE SECRETARY OF THE NAVY

### The Confederate Navy

The Navy was established by the Confederate Congress on February 21, 1861. President Jefferson Davis appointed forty-nine year old lawyer, Stephen Russell Mallory of Pensacola, Florida, to become the Secretary of Navy, a post that he held throughout the war. Davis had served with Mallory in the U.S. Senate from 1851 to 1861. During that time, Mallory served as Chairman of the Naval Affairs Committee. In that capacity, Mallory kept abreast of naval improvements around the world.

When Florida seceded, Mallory came home to Pensacola and was there when word came of his appointment.

The Navy was responsible for protecting the Southern harbors and coastlines, making the sea lanes of commerce difficult for the United States by attacking merchant vessels worldwide, and breaking the Federal blockade by forcing U.S. Navy ships to withdraw from blockade duty to pursue the Confederate raiders.

In 1861, the Confederate Navy was non-existent with the exception of the almost destroyed and abandoned Federal navy installations at Norfolk, Virginia, and Pensacola, Florida. The Charleston Navy Base was taken over by South Carolina troops intact before hostilities actually began.

The South was without naval facilities or port equipment. Not a single marine engine could be manufactured in the South. When the war began, the Navy consisted of thirty ships of which only fourteen were seaworthy.

At the start of the war, there were sixteen Southern captains, thirty-four commanders, seventy-six lieutenants, and 111 midshipmen present for duty. In every ship, without exception, Southern officers returned their ships to their home ports before resigning their commissions. From these officers and men that came from nearly every Confederate State (Florida's share was almost 2,000 men), Secretary Mallory built the Confederate Navy. The demand for more officers was solved by the establishment of the Confederate Naval Academy on board the CSS *Patrick Henry* anchored in the James River.

On May 10, 1861, Mallory urged the construction of an iron-clad Confederate Navy to off-set the superiority of the Federal Navy. He stated that the Confederate Navy must have quality, strength, and invulnerability.

Under Mallory's leadership, his staff, including Captain James D. Bullock and Lieutenant James H. North, negotiated for the purchase of three English sail and steam cruisers.

The first was the CSS *Florida* commanded by Captain James Newland Maffitt, who, despite neutrality problems with British and Spanish authorities and a bout with yellow fever, sailed his ship to Mobile to complete its outfitting as a ship of war. On the night of January 15, 1863, the *Florida* finally broke out onto the high seas to become a terror to Federal merchant vessels. After seven months of raiding, Maffitt put his ship into dock at Brest, France where he asked to be relieved. The *Florida* captured fifty-five prizes and sank many other ships carrying goods to the Federal Army. Maffitt was succeeded by Commander Joseph N. Barney and a few weeks later by Lieutenant Charles M. Morris.

On October 4, 1863, the ship put into Bahia, Brazil, and anchored near the *USS Waschusett*, assuming safety under the rules of international warfare. The Southern crew of officers and men went ashore. The Federals committed an act of international outrage against the neutral nation of Brazil and seized the *CSS Florida* in the harbor. The *Florida* was lost after a collision in the Chesapeake Bay. Brazil received only an apology.

The second sail and steam cruiser delivered to the Confederacy by British sympathizers was the *CSS Alabama* commanded by Captain Raphael Semmes, who took command of the ship in the Azores. During the next twenty-two months, (from August 1862 to June 1864) the *Alabama* captured and sank more enemy ships (a total of ninety-two) than any other Confederate raider. She even sank the *USS Hatteras* in a thirteen minute battle off of the coast of Galveston, Texas.

In June 1862, Semmes brought the *Alabama* into Cherbourg, France for repairs. Shortly after his arrival, the USS *Kearsarge* appeared off Cherbourg and, after being challenged by Captain Semmes, gave battle outside the port. In a battle that lasted a little over an hour, the *Alabama* was sunk. Semmes was taken away to England by a private yacht.

The third sail and steam cruiser delivered to the Confederacy was the CSS *Shenandoah* commanded by Captain James Iredell Waddell. The *Shenandoah* joined the Confederate Navy on October 19, 1864. On a cruise to Australia, the *Shenandoah* captured thirty-six prizes.

After repairs in Melbourne in January and February 1865, Waddell sailed the Pacific, sinking and rounding up more prizes. He sailed on into the Bering Sea and the Arctic Ocean where the *Shenandoah* virtually destroyed the Union whaling fleet. On June 28, 1865, Waddell scored the last victories against eleven New England whalers. A Confederate naval officer from one of the boarding boats drew his pistol and fired a warning shot thus becoming the last shot to be fired in the War for Southern Independence.

In August 1865, Waddell learned from the British bark *HMS Barracouta* that the war was over. Although he was sailing down the west coast of North America, Waddell contemplated an attack on San Francisco. Instead he sailed south and removed his cannons so as not to be taken by Union warships and hung as pirates. After rounding Cape Horn, he decided to sail for Liverpool rather than Cape Town which would have been closer.

As the CSS *Shenandoah* sailed toward the North Atlantic, they made their fourth crossing of the equator in 110 degree heat. On October 28, 1865, Confederate Marine Corps Sergeant George Canning died becoming the last active duty casualty.

On November 6, 1865, the *Shenandoah* entered the Mersey River and anchored astern of HMS *Donegal*. Waddell formally surrendered to Captain Paynter of the *Donegal* and the *Shenandoah* lowered her flag for the last time – the last Confederate combat unit to do so.

Collectively, these three Confederate cruisers sank, burned, or captured almost 200 Federal ships forcing the Federal Navy to assign some of its ships from the blockade to protect their merchant marine. The loss of Federal shipping forced Marine Insurance Underwritersand ship owners to bring pressure on the Lincoln government for an end of the war.

Iron-clad rams were under construction for the Confederate Navy by the Lairds of Birkenhead and in other British shipyards. Pressure from the Lincoln government eventually forced Lord John Russell to enforce Britain's neutrality laws, seize the rams, and turn them over to the British Navy.

Mallory encouraged the development of the torpedo or marine mine, which was a magazine of powder equipped with a detonator. The Navy used anchored torpedoes to mine harbors at New Orleans and at Mobile; as well as other harbors along the entire coastline. More than thirty Federal ships were sunk by torpedoes during the war.

It was through Mallory's efforts that private marine engineers built and launched four successful submarines from 1862 to 1864. The CSS *Pioneer* was built by McClintock and Watson in New Orleans only to be scuttled in April 1862 in Lake Pontchartrain to prevent her from falling into enemy hands when New Orleans was over taken. A sister ship was built in Mobile and lost at sea during bad weather.

The CSS *H.L. Hunley* was also built in Mobile and shipped to Charleston by railcar to expedite the defenses of that city. She sank twice, drowning her crew of five each time. She was raised and put back into service. On the night of February 17, 1864, she crashed her torpedo against the hull of the *USS Housatonic,* the Federal steam sloop of war. The *Hunley* sank near her target, carrying her crew with her. The *Hunley* was the last American submarine to sink an enemy warship until World War II.

Mallory also experimented with and perfected the CSS *David*, an iron torpedo boat built in Charleston in 1863. The 50'-0" long, cigar shaped steamer was operated by a crew of four and was capable of a maximum speed of seven knots. The *David* was armed with a torpedo, which carried 100 pounds of explosives connected to a ten foot spar at the bow. There were several other torpedo boats built and operated in and around the port of Charleston. They damaged Federal ships, but failed to sink a single ship.

After the Confederate occupation of the abandoned Norfolk Navy Yard, the scuttled USS *Merrimac,* now renamed the CSS *Virginia,* was brought into service. The *Virginia* was originally a wooden frigate that was burned at the water's edge and sunk by the Federals. She was raised and rebuilt inside; strengthened in every way and armored with such iron as could be obtained. A slanting deck house was constructed, and an iron bow or beak was added for ramming purposes.

To the able Confederate Naval ship designers: Chief Engineer William P. Williamson, Lieutenant John L. Porter (Chief Naval Constructor), and to Lieutenant John M. Brooke (the inventor of the Brooke rifled gun) goes the credit for assisting Mallory in introducing the iron-clad battle ship into Naval Warfare history. Brooke placed the guns on the *Virginia*. There was one seven inch pivotal Brooke rifle at each end and eight guns, four to the side and six of the eight were nine-inch Dahlgren plus two more 32-pound rifles. Her speed was about five knots. She required twenty-two feet of water under her keel to clear the bottom.

The *Virginia* was commanded by Flag Officer, Captain Franklin Buchanan and carried a crew of 325 officers and men. She had never been given a complete trial run on the day of her initial baptism of fire. Even her gun crews were fresh from the Confederate Army Artillery units. They did not know their officers and had never fired a gun together. The ship was hard to steer.

The Confederate flotilla that moved towards Hampton Roads from the Norfolk Navy base consisted of the *Virginia*, the *Patrick Henry*, the *Jamestown*, the *Teaser*, the *Raleigh*, and the *Beaufort*. Midshipman Mallory, the son of the Secretary, was to see action for the first time on the *Beaufort*.

On the morning of March 9, 1862, the *Monitor* and the *Virginia* fought for four hours mercilessly, but ineffectively. The *Virginia* rammed the USS *Cumberland* and sank her. When the *Virginia* reversed engines, she left most of the iron ram wedged into the *Cumberland*. She then attacked the USS *Congress* and ran her aground. Next, came the battle with the *Monitor*.

Early in the afternoon, the *Virginia* turned towards Norfolk leaving the *Monitor* in possession of Hampton Roads. After the Federals re-occupied the Norfolk Navy Yard, the *Virginia* was scuttled on to prevent capture.

When the war ended, Mallory left Richmond with Davis and the other cabinet members. On May 20, 1865, he was taken prisoner at LaGrange, Georgia en route to Pensacola and imprisoned at Fort Lafayette, New York. He was released in March, 1866.

He returned to Pensacola where he practiced law until his death on November 9, 1873.

The entire world and especially the naval forces owe Mallory their gratitude for his efforts in bringing naval warfare to a more perfect state than ever before.

At the end of the war, the Confederate Navy consisted of 315 ships of which 104 were gunboats. The Confederate blockade runners consisted of 101 ships and cruisers, such as the *Shenandoah,* numbered twenty-two ships. There were nine torpedo boats plus twenty-five iron-clad rams – all this put into service in four years. The Navy also ended the war with three submarines.

# 24
## GOVERNOR JOHN MILTON

John Milton was born in Jefferson County, Georgia, on April 20, 1807. He fought in the Second Seminole War (1835-1842). In 1846, he moved and settled in Jackson County near Marianna, where he became a successful farmer and politician.

He was a strong supporter of states rights and was an early advocate for secession. He was a delegate to the 1860 Democrat National Convention, and, in the same year, ran for governor on the Democrat secessionist ticket. He was elected the fifth Governor of Florida.

He assumed office on October 7, 1861, and immediately had to deal with the issue of keeping enough troops in the state to guard its coastline or to send this valuable resource to the Confederate Army where Florida's manpower was sorely needed. Milton knew Federal troops would eventually invade Florida because of its strategic importance and supply of foodstuffs, but he also realized that the Confederacy needed Florida troops more. So, he acquiesced to Richmond's demands.

Milton cooperated fully with the Confederate government in Richmond, unlike many other Southern governors who were considered obstructionists by withholding troops, arms, and ammunition. The cooperation wasn't reciprocal, however, because Richmond didn't believe that the Florida coastline was vital enough to send troops to protect it.

No Southern governor surpassed, nor few equaled, the devotion and service Milton rendered the Confederacy. During the war, President Jefferson Davis wrote Milton:

*It is gratifying to me to be able to say to you that in this time of our great trouble, when so many are disposed to withhold from the Confederate Government the means of success, you should occupy the high standpoint of strengthening its hands by all the means in your power and of nobly disregarding all considerations except the common wealth.*

Federal forces occupied St. Augustine, Fernandina, and Jacksonville by March 1862. Of more crucial strategic importance was the port of Apalachicola which was sheltered by a chain of offshore islands. The Apalachicola River provided a link with the Alabama and Georgia interior and an outlet to the Gulf of Mexico for Confederate ships that slipped by the Federal blockade. Scarcely less important was the area's ability to produce large quantities of salt.

Milton adamantly maintained that Apalachicola should be defended to the last extremity. No less a military expert than General Robert E. Lee concurred. However, before Southern troops could act on his orders to secure the area, eight Union boats captured Apalachicola on April 3, 1862.

On May 20, 1862, a boat carrying twenty-one men left the blockading vessel and approached the shore. They were fired upon by Confederates under Captain H.T. Blocker of the Beauregard Rangers. Seventeen of the boat's occupants were either killed or wounded. There were no Confederate casualties. The port continued to change hands repeatedly throughout the war, usually without serious conflict.

Milton directed operations from Tallahassee. Since the city was dangerously within striking distance of Federal troops, he sent his eleven children (the youngest whom he had named Jeff Davis) to his Jackson County plantation, Sylvania.

The major offensive Milton expected came on February 20, 1864. At Olustee, a Southern force halted the westward advance of the enemy. Slightly more than a year later, Confederates turned back Union forces at Natural Bridge on March 5, 1865, and saved the capital from capture. A month later, Lee surrendered to General Ulysses S. Grant at Appomattox Court House.

Several days earlier, Milton had, in complete despair, put down his executive duties and traveled to Sylvania. On April 1, tired and depressed, the governor committed suicide. Floridians were left to ponder the words he had uttered in his last address to the Florida Legislature that death would be preferable to reunion.

He was buried in the St. Luke's Episcopal Church cemetery. On May 10, less than six weeks after Milton died, Federal troops entered Tallahassee without opposition.

The Florida that remained was not the same state it was when Milton became governor. The state's population of more than 62,000 slaves was now free. Florida's political parties were divided on a course of action, and the plantation aristocracy was dismantled. Floridians endured shortages of food and clothing. Reconstruction would take a severe toll.

# 25

## GOVERNOR MADISON STARKE PERRY

Perry was Florida's fourth elected governor and served from 1856 until 1861. Born in 1814 in Lancaster County, South Carolina, he was the youngest child of Benjamin Perry and Mary Starke. In 1845, he migrated to Florida, settling in Alachua County where he helped to establish the town of Rochelle. He was soon recognized as a leading figure among the plantation owners and, in 1849, was elected to represent the county in the Florida House of Representatives. The following year he was elected to the Florida Senate.

In 1856, Perry ran for governor and was sworn in on October 5, 1857. As governor, he helped resolve the long standing boundary dispute with the State of Georgia and encouraged the building of railroads in the state. As the governors before him, Perry anticipated the possibility of secession. In 1858, he called for the reformation of the state's militia and the purchase of weapons in the event the militia was called to duty. Florida seceded from the Union on January 11, 1861, and Perry called for the evacuation of all Federal troops from Florida and their replacement by Florida militia.

After his term as governor, Perry served the Confederacy as a colonel in the 7th Florida Infantry Regiment until he became ill. He was forced to resign on April 30, 1863. He returned to his plantation in Rochelle. Perry died in March 1865. He was buried in the Oak Ridge Cemetery in Rochelle. He was survived by his wife and two children.

# 26
## GENERAL E. KIRBY SMITH

Edmund Kirby Smith was born on May 16, 1824, in St. Augustine, Florida, to Joseph Lee Smith and Frances Kirby. Kirby Smith's parents had moved from Connecticut to Florida in 1821.

Kirby Smith attended the United States Military Academy at West Point where he gained the nicknamed Seminole for his native state. He graduated in 1845, twenty-fifth in a class of forty-one cadets and was commissioned a brevet second lieutenant in the 5th U.S. Infantry. He served in the Mexican War under the command of General Zachary Taylor at the Battle of Palo Alto and the Battle of Resaca de la Palma. Under General Winfield Scott, he received a brevet promotion to first lieutenant for gallant and meritorious service at the Battle of Cerro Gordo. He was again brevetted for to captain for gallant and meritorious conduct at the battles of Contreras and Churubusco.

Kirby Smith served with his older brother, Ephraim, a captain in the 5th U.S. Infantry. Ephraim died from wounds suffered at the Battle of Molino del Rey in 1847.

From 1849 to 1852, Kirby Smith taught mathematics at West Point. After his stint at West Pont, he served as a captain in the 2nd U.S. Cavalry, primarily in Texas, fighting Indians. In 1859, he was wounded in the Nescutunga Valley of Texas. When Texas seceded, Kirby Smith, now a major, refused to surrender his command at Camp Colorado (in what is today Coleman, Texas) to the Texas State forces under Benjamin McCulloch. He demonstrated his willingness to fight and hold his command.

Kirby Smith wrote to Florida Governor Madison Perry on January 12, 1861, offering his services. He tendered his resignation from the 2nd U.S. Cavalry on March 3, which became effective on April 6. He set out for Florida, but on the way, met with several senior officers with whom he had served. He asked them to write the Confederate Secretary of War on his behalf. Judge Benjamin A. Putnam, Kirby Smith's uncle, wrote to President Jefferson Davis. All of this led to Kirby Smith being initially commissioned a major in the regular artillery on March 16, 1861.

On April 20, 1861, he was transferred to the regular cavalry as a lieutenant colonel. He received orders to Virginia and served as Assistant Adjutant General on the staff of General Joseph Eggleston Johnston. Kirby Smith was promoted to brigadier general on June 17, 1861, and served as Johnston's chief of staff during the planning of the First Battle of Manassas.

On July 2, 1861, he took command of a brigade composed of the 9th, 10th, and 11th Alabama, 14th Mississippi, and 38th Virginia. He subsequently commanded the brigades of Elsey and Forney and led them during the battle. Kirby Smith was severely wounded in the neck and shoulder. Family lore has it that while recovering from his wounds, he met and married the girl who had made him a shirt on the joking promise that whoever made the garment would get the handsome colonel who went with it. The handsome colonel was actually a general but with the similarity of emblems, it is easy to understand how this mistake could be made.

After he recovered from his wounds, Kirby Smith was responsible for the Department of Florida for twelve days before Johnston requested that he become his chief of staff.

In March 1862, Kirby Smith traveled to Knoxville to assume command of the Department of East Tennessee and Kentucky, North Georgia, Western North Carolina, including the infantry divisions of Stevenson, McCown, and Heth, and cavalry brigades of Forrest, Morgan, Scott, and Ashby. Together with General Braxton Bragg, he undertook the invasion of Kentucky. After scoring a victory at Richmond, Kentucky on August 30, (he received Congress' thanks on

February 17, 1864, for his actions at Richmond) he was named to the newly created position of lieutenant general, becoming a corps commander in the Army of Tennessee. He then joined Bragg for the battle of Perryville. He had difficulties with Bragg on a number of issues and asked to be detached with his own command, which was refused. Finally, on February 9, 1863, he was given command of the Trans-Mississippi Department, which included the District of Louisiana. When Vicksburg fell in July, this area was cut off from the War Department and became for all purposes a separate command (known as Kirby Smithdom).

Smith was promoted to the rank of full general on February 19, 1864, one of only seven men in the Confederacy to achieve this rank.

In the spring of 1864, General Richard Taylor, directly under Smith's command, soundly defeated General Nathaniel P. Banks at the Battle of Mansfield in the Red River Campaign. After the Battle of Pleasant Hill on April 9, 1864, Smith joined Taylor and dispatched half of Taylor's army under the command of General George Walker northward to defeat General Frederick Steele's incursion into Arkansas. This decision was strongly opposed by Taylor, and because of the continued disagreement between the two generals, Taylor was put in a separate command.

Smith attempted to send reinforcements east of the Mississippi River, but, as in the case of his earlier attempts to relieve Vicksburg, it proved impossible because of the Union Navy's control of the river. In response, Kirby Smith sent General Sterling Price with all remaining cavalry to invade Missouri, which resulted in the war in the west becoming one of small raids and guerrilla activity.

Smith appointed a number of generals, but under Confederate law, the president alone was authorized to make such appointments. Davis repudiated Smith's appointments, but later confirmed a few of them.

By early May 1865, no regular Confederate troops remained east of the Mississippi River. Kirby Smith received official proposals that the surrender of his department be negotiated. The Federals intimated that terms could be loose, but Kirby-Smith's demands were considered unrealistic. Kirby Smith considered continuing the fight and Lieutenant General U. S. Grant took preliminary steps to invade West Texas should it prove necessary. It did not.

The war's last fight took place on May 12th and 13th at Palmito Ranch where 350 Confederates under Colonel John S. "Rest in Peace" Ford was victorious over 800 Federals under the command of Colonel Theodore H. Barrett. Afterwards the Confederates learned that Richmond had fallen and that General Robert E. Lee had surrendered more than a month earlier. This news devastated the morale of everyone, and the troop's abandoned their lines. A similar loss of morale occurred throughout the department.

On May 18th, Kirby Smith left by stagecoach for Houston with plans to rally the remnants of his department's troops. While he traveled, the last of the department's army dissolved. On May 26, at New Orleans, Lieutenant General Simon B. Buckner, acting in Kirby Smith's name surrendered the department. Kirby Smith reached Houston on May 27th and learned that he had no troops.

Not all of the Trans-Mississippi Confederates went home, some 2,000 went to Mexico, most alone or in small groups, but one body numbered 300. With them, mounted on a mule, wearing a calico shirt and silk kerchief, sporting a revolver strapped to his hip and a shotgun on his saddle, was Kirby Smith. Reaching Mexico, he decided to travel on to Cuba.

Returning to the United States in November 1865, he was initially the president of an insurance and telegraph company (which was unsuccessful), and then the president of the University of Nashville from 1870 to 1875. Having considered at periods throughout his life becoming an Episcopal minister, he decided that he was too old to embark upon this course. He taught mathematics for eighteen years at the University of the South at Sewanee, Tennessee.

He and his wife raised eleven children, something that should give pause to any young lady volunteering to make shirts in wartime.

The family name has been a subject of much speculation, but perhaps Joseph Howard Parks in *General Edmund Kirby Smith, C.S.A.,* is the most authoritative source. Kirby Smith's father gave Edmund and his older brother, Ephraim, their mother's maiden name, Kirby, as a middle name. Ephraim, had been called Kirby. But Edmund, who was more often called Ted by his family and Seminole by his West Point classmates, took to signing his war reports in the spring of 1861 as E. Kirby Smith to distinguish himself from the other Smiths. The family then became known, as the General became famous, as the Kirby-Smiths. The hyphenation between Kirby and Smith happened after his death. He is generally indexed alphabetically under Smith, Edmund Kirby. Apparently, he never considered Kirby as part of his surname.

# BIBLIOGRAPHY

The original bibliography was compiled by Gene H. Kizer, Jr. and has been modified by Ben H. Willingham to reflect certain additional events not covered in the original work. See the bibliography following this chronology for complete information on every source, especially primary sources. The following sources were used repeatedly: Ralph A. Wooster, *The Secession Conventions of the South* (Princeton, NJ: Princeton University Press, 1962); Charles W. Ramsdell, "Lincoln and Fort Sumter," *Journal of Southern History*, Volume 3, Issue 3 (Aug., 1937); E. B. Long with Barbara Long, *The Civil War Day by Day, An Almanac, 1861 - 1865* (New York: Da Capo Press, 1971; reprint, New York, Da Capo Press, 1985); John Amasa May and Joan Reynolds Faunt, *South Carolina Secedes* (Columbia, SC: University of South Carolina Press, 1962); *The War of the Rebellion: A Compilation of the Official Records of the Union and Confederate Armies* (Washington: Government Printing Office, 1900; reprint, Historical Times, Inc., 1985); W. Buck Yearns, ed., *The Confederate Governors* (Athens, GA: The University of Georgia Press, 1985); John Shipley Tilley, *Lincoln Takes Command* (second printing, Nashville: Bill Coats, Ltd., 1991).

Bibliography Primary Sources:

Ackroyd, Peter. *Dickens*. London: 1990, 271, in Charles Adams, *When in the Course of Human Events, Arguing the Case for Southern Secession*. Lanham: Rowman & Littlefield Publishers, Inc., 2000, 89.

Adams, Charles, *When in the Course of Human Events, Arguing the Case for Southern Secession*. Lanham: Rowman & Littlefield Publishers, Inc., 2000.

Address of the People of South Carolina, Assembled in Convention, to the People of the Slaveholding States of the United States, adopted December 24, 1860, by the South Carolina Secession Convention, Charleston, S.C., in John Amasa May and Joan Reynolds Faunt, *South Carolina Secedes*. Columbia: University of South Carolina Press, 1960.

# Bibliography

Address to the people of Texas, March 30, 1861, in *The War of the Rebellion: A Compilation of the Official Records of the Union and Confederate Armies.* Washington: Government Printing Office, 1900; reprint, Historical Times, Inc., 1985, Series IV, Volume 1.

Allen, John J. "The Botetourt Resolutions of Judge John J. Allen," delivered and adopted with only two dissenting votes in a mass public meeting in Botetourt County, Virginia, 10 December 1860, in *Southern Historical Society Papers.* Reprint, Broadfoot Publishing Company, Morningside Bookshop, 1990, Volume 1, January-June, 1876.

Beard, Charles A., and Beard, Mary R. *The Rise of American Civilization.* New York: The MacMillan Company, 1936.

Benjamin, Judah P. "Farewell Address to the U. S. Senate," delivered February 5, 1861, by Louisiana Senator Judah P. Benjamin in the U. S. Senate in Edwin Anderson Alderman and Joel Chandler Harris, eds., *Library of Southern Literature.* Atlanta: The Martin and Hoyt Company, 1907.

Benning, Henry L., "Henry L. Benning's Secessionist Speech, Monday Evening, November 19," delivered in Milledgeville, Georgia, November 19, 1860, in William W. Freehling and Craig M. Simpson, *Secession Debated, Georgia's Showdown in 1860.* New York: Oxford University Press, 1992.

Benson, Lee. "Explanations of American Civil War Causation" in *Toward the Scientific Study of History.* Philadelphia: J. B. Lippincott, 1972, 246, 295-303, in Gavin Wright, *The Political Economy of the Cotton South, Households, Markets, and Wealth in the Nineteenth Century.* New York: W. W. Norton & Company, 1978, 136.

"Boston Transcript, The, March 18, 1861," in Adams, *When in the Course of Human Events, Arguing the Case for Southern Secession.* Lanham: Rowman & Littlefield Publishers, Inc., 2000, 65.

Brown, Joseph E. "Special Message of Governor Joseph E. Brown on Federal Relations, delivered to the Georgia Senate and House of Representatives in Milledgeville, Georgia, on November 7, 1860," in Allen D. Chandler, *The Confederate Records of the State of Georgia,* Volume I, Atlanta: Charles P. Byrd, State Printer, 1909.

Buchanan, James. "Republican Fanaticism as a Cause of the Civil War," in Edwin C. Rozwenc, ed., *The Causes of the American Civil War.* Boston: D. C. Heath and Company, 1961.

Calhoun, John C. "A Discourse on the Constitution," in Richard Cralle, ed., *The Works of John C. Calhoun.* New York: D. Appleton and Company, 1851-1856, Volume 1, 349-52.

Calhoun, John C. "Letter to John McLean, August 4, 1828," in Meriwether et al., eds., *The Papers of John C. Calhoun,* Vol. X, 407, in James L. Huston, "Property Rights in Slavery and the Coming of the Civil War." *Journal of Southern History,* Volume LXV, Number 2, May, 1999, 270.

Campbell, John A. "Memoranda Relative to the Secession Movement in 1860-61," in "The Papers of Hon. John A. Campbell--1861-1865," *Southern Historical Society Papers,* New Series--Number IV, Volume XLII, September, 1917. Richmond: James Power Smith, Secretary; reprint, Broadfoot Publishing Company and Morningside Bookshop, 1991.

*Chicago Times,* The, "Value of the Union," December 10, 1860, in Howard Cecil Perkins, ed., *Northern Editorials on Secession.* Gloucester: Peter Smith, 1964, Volume II, 573-574.

Clopton, David. "Letter of Commissioner David Clopton of Alabama to Delaware Governor William Burton," in *The War of the Rebellion: A*

# Bibliography

*Compilation of the Official Records of the Union and Confederate Armies.* Washington: Government Printing Office, 1900; reprint, Historical Times, Inc., 1985, Series IV, Volume 1.

Cobb, Thomas R. R. "Thomas R. R. Cobb's Secessionist Speech, Monday Evening, November 12," delivered to the Georgia legislature in Milledgeville, 12 November 1860, in William W. Freehling and Craig M. Simpson, *Secession Debated, Georgia's Showdown in 1860.* New York: Oxford University Press, 1992.

Cobb, Williamson R. W. "Personal Explanation of the Hon. W. R. W. Cobb, of Alabama," delivered in the United States House of Representatives, January 7, 1861. Washington: W. H. Moore, 1861. *Commercial Advertiser, Courier and Enquirer, Post, Herald, News, and Journal of Commerce,* March 1, 1861, in Philip S. Foner, *Business & Slavery, The New York Merchants & the Irrepressible Conflict.* Chapel Hill: The University of North Carolina Press, 1941, 278. Concurrent resolutions tendering aid to the President of the United States in support of the Constitution and the Union, passed by the New York State Assembly, January 11, 1861, in The *New York Times,* January 12, 1861.

Cohn, David L. *The Life and Times of King Cotton.* New York: Oxford University Press, 1956.

"Confederate Constitution of 1861," *An Inquiry into American Constitutionalism.* Columbia: University of Missouri Press, 1991, 72.

*Cornhill Magazine,* "The Dissolution of the Union," 4, (July-October 1861), 153, in Charles Adams, *When in the Course of Human Events, Arguing the Case for Southern Secession.* Lanham: Rowman & Littlefield Publishers, Inc., 2000, 72.

Coward, Barry. *The Stuart Age, England, 1603-1714,* Second Edition, London: Longman Group, Ltd., 1994.

Crist, Lynda Lasswell, ed. *The Papers of Jefferson Davis.* Baton Rouge: Louisiana State University Press, 1992, Volume 7.

Current, Richard N. *The Lincoln Nobody Knows.* New York: McGraw-Hill Book Company, Inc., 1958.

Davis, Jefferson, Senator. "Farewell Address," to the United States Senate, 21 January 1861, in Lynda Lasswell Crist, ed., *The Papers of Jefferson Davis.* Baton Rouge: Louisiana State University Press, 1992, Volume 7. "Inaugural Address" as Provisional President of the Confederate States of America, 18 February 1861, at Montgomery, Alabama, in Lynda Lasswell Crist, ed., *The Papers of Jefferson Davis.* Baton Rouge: Louisiana State University Press, 1992, Volume 7.

DeRosa, Marshall L. *The Confederate Constitution of 1861, An Inquiry into American Constitutionalism.* Columbia: University of Missouri Press, 1991.

DeRosa, Marshall L., ed., *The Politics of Dissolution, The Quest for a National Identity & the American Civil War.* New Brunswick: Transaction Publishers, 1998.

Dobson, John M. *Two Centuries of Tariffs: The Background and Emergence of the U.S. International Trade Commission.* Washington: United States International Trade Commission, 1976.

"Declaration of Causes which Impel the State of Texas to Secede from the Federal Union," adopted February 2, 1861, by the Texas Secession Convention, Austin, Texas, in E. W. Winkler, ed., *Journal of the Secession Convention of Texas,* Austin: 1912.

"Declaration of the Immediate Causes Which Induce and Justify the Secession of South Carolina from the Federal Union," adopted December 24, 1860, by the South Carolina Secession Convention, Charleston, S.C., in John Amasa May and Joan Reynolds Faunt, South *Carolina Secedes.* Columbia: University of South Carolina Press, 1960.

# Bibliography

"Declaration of the Immediate Causes Which Induce and Justify the Secession of the State of Mississippi from the Federal Union," adopted January 26, 1861, by the Mississippi Secession Convention, in *Journal of the State Convention*. Jackson: E. Barksdale, State Printer, 1861.

Dickens, Charles. "American Disunion," in Charles Adams, *When in the Course of Human Events, Arguing the Case for Southern Secession*. Lanham: Rowman & Littlefield Publishers, Inc., 2000, 90-91.

Faust, Patricia L., ed. *Historical Times Illustrated Encyclopedia of the Civil War*. New York: Harper & Row, Publishers, 1986.

Foner, Philip S. *Business & Slavery, The New York Merchants & the Irrepressible Conflict*. Chapel Hill: The University of North Carolina Press, 1941.

Freehling, William W. and Craig M. Simpson. *Secession Debated, Georgia's Showdown in 1860*. New York: Oxford University Press, 1992.

Greeley, Horace. *The American Conflict*. Hartford: O. D. Case and Company, 1865, Volume 1, 438-439, in William C. Wright, *The Secession Movement in the Middle Atlantic States*. Rutherford: Fairleigh Dickinson University Press, 1973, 14.

Guilds, John Caldwell. *Simms, A Literary Life*. Fayetteville: The University of Arkansas Press, 1992.

Hale, S. F. "Letter of Commissioner S. F. Hale of Alabama to Kentucky Governor B. Magoffin, December 27, 1860," in *The War of the Rebellion: A Compilation of the Official Records of the Union and Confederate Armies*. Washington: Government Printing Office, 1900; reprint, Historical Times, Inc., 1985, Series IV, Volume 1.

Helper, Hinton Rowan. *The Impending Crisis of the South: How to Meet It*. Reprint, New York: Collier Books, 1963.

"History and Debates of the Convention of The People of Alabama," William R. Smith, Delegate, ed. *The History and Debates of the Convention of The People of Alabama.* Montgomery: White, Pfister & Co., 1861; reprint, Spartanburg: The Reprint Company, Publishers, 1975.

Hummel, Jeffrey Rogers. *Emancipating Slaves, Enslaving Free Men, A History of the American Civil War.* Chicago: Open Court, 1996.

Huston, James L. *The Panic of 1857 and the Coming of the Civil War.* Baton Rouge: Louisiana State University Press, 1987.

Huston, James L. "Property Rights in Slavery and the Coming of the Civil War," *Journal of Southern History,* Volume LXV, Number 2, May, 1999.

Huston, James L. *Securing the Fruits of Labor, The American Concept of Wealth Distribution, 1765-1900.* Baton Rouge: Louisiana State University Press, 1998.

Jamison, David F. "Opening Speech by then Temporary President of the South Carolina Secession Convention, General David F. Jamison, December 17, 1860, in the First Baptist Church in Columbia, South Carolina," in John Amasa May and Joan Reynolds Faunt, *South Carolina Secedes.* Columbia: University of South Carolina Press, 1960.

Jefferson, Thomas. "A Summary View of the Rights of British America," 1774, in James L. Huston, *Securing the Fruits of Labor, The American Concept of Wealth Distribution, 1765-1900.* Baton Rouge: Louisiana State University Press, 1998, 17.

"Joint Resolutions of the General Assembly of Alabama, adopted February 24, 1860," in William R. Smith, Delegate, *The History and Debates of the Convention of The People of Alabama.* Montgomery: White, Pfister & Co., 1861; reprint, Spartanburg, SC: The Reprint Company, Publishers, 1975.

Kettell, Thomas Prentice. *Southern Wealth and Northern Profits, as Exhibited in Statistical Facts and Offical (sic) Figures: Showing the Necessity of Union to the Future Prosperity and Welfare of the Republic.* Original edition, New York: Geo. W. & John A. Wood, 1860; reprint, University, AL: University of Alabama Press, 1965.

Letcher, John. "Governor John Letcher's Message on Federal Relations to the legislature of Virginia in extraordinary secession on 7 January 1861," in *Journal of the House of Delegates of the State of Virginia, for the Extra Session, 1861.* Richmond: William F. Ritchie, Public Printer, 1861, Document I.

"Letter to W. W. De Cerjat, March 16, 1862," in Graham Storey, Ed., *The Letters of Charles Dickens.* Oxford: Clarendon Press, 1998, Volume Ten, 1862-1864.

Lincoln, Abraham. "A House Divided," delivered 16 June 1858, at the end of the Republican State Convention, Springfield, Illinois, in Roy P. Basler, ed., *The Collected Works of Abraham Lincoln*, History Book Club edition. New Brunswick: Rutgers University Press, 1953, Volume II. "Campaign Circular from Whig Committee," March 4, 1843, in Roy P. Basler,   ed., *The Collected Works of Abraham Lincoln*, History Book Club edition. New Brunswick: Rutgers University Press, 1953, Volume I. "First Inaugural Address," 4 March 1861, in Sheldon Vanauken, *The Glittering Illusion, English Sympathy for the Southern Confederacy.* Regnery Gateway: Washington: 1989, 35. "Letter to Francis P. Blair, December 21, 1860," in E. B. Long with Barbara Long, *The Civil War Day by Day, An Almanac 1861-1865.* New York: Da Capo Press, 1971; reprint, New York: Da Capo Press, 1985. "Letter to Lyman Trumbull, December 10, 1860," in Earl Schenck Miers, ed., *Lincoln Day by Day, A Chronology, 1809-1865.* Washington: Lincoln Sesquicentennial Commission, 1960, Volume II, 1849-1860. "The Seventh Lincoln-Douglas Debate," 15 October 1858, in Don E. Fehrenbacher, ed., *Abraham Lincoln, Speeches and Writings, 1832-1858.* New York: Library Classics of the United States, Inc., 1989. *Liverpool Daily Post,* 11 March 1862, in

Locke, John. "The Second Treatise of Government," in Peter Laslett, *John Locke, Two Treatises of Government, A Critical Edition with an Introduction and Apparatus Criticus,* Second Edition. Cambridge: University Press, 1970, 309, 399-400.

*London Times, The,* November 7, 1861, in Jeffrey Rogers Hummel, *Emancipating Slaves, Enslaving Free Men, A History of the American Civil War.* Chicago: Open Court, 1996.

Long, E. B. with Long, Barbara. *The Civil War Day by Day, An Almanac 1861-1865.* New York: Da Capo Press, 1971; reprint, New York: Da Capo Press, 1985.

Lloyd, Christopher. *The Navy and the Slave Trade. London, 1949,* 163, in Brian Jenkins, *Britain & the War for the Union.* London: McGill's-Queen's University Press, 1974, Volume 1, 75. May, John Amasa and Joan Reynolds Faunt. South Carolina Secedes. Columbia: University of South Carolina Press, 1960.

*Manchester (N.H.) Union Democrat,* "Let Them Go!", editorial, 19 February 1861, in Howard Cecil Perkins, *Northern Editorials on Secession.* Gloucester: Peter Smith, 1964, Volume II, 592.

Marx, Karl. "The North American Civil War," in Karl Marx and Frederick Engels, *The Civil War in the United States.* Reprint: New York: International Publishers, 1971, 58.

Marx, Karl and Engels, Frederick. *The Civil War in the United States.* Reprint: New York: International Publishers, 1971.

McManus, Edgar J. *Black Bondage in the North.* New York: Syracuse University Press, 1973.

Miller, John. *The Glorious Revolution,* Second Edition. London: Longman, 1997.

Morse, H. Newcomb. "The Foundations and Meaning of Secession," *Stetson Law Review of Stetson University College of Law,* Volume. XV, No. 2, 1986.

# Bibliography

Moore, Thomas O. "Extracts from the Message of the Governor of Louisiana to the State Legislature, January 22, 1861," in *The War of the Rebellion: A Compilation of the Official Records of the Union and Confederate Armies.* Washington: Government Printing Office, 1880, Series I, Volume 1.

"Morrill Tariff, The" All the Year Round, December 28, 1861, 328-330, in Charles Adams, *When in the Course of Human Events, Arguing the Case for Southern Secession.* Lanham: Rowman & Littlefield Publishers, Inc., 2000, 90-91.

Nelson, Thomas A. R. "Minority Report of the Committee of Thirty-three" of the United States House of Representatives. Washington: H. Polkinhorn, 1861. "Speech of Hon. Thomas A. R. Nelson, of Tennessee, On the Disturbed Condition of the Country." Washington: H. Polkinhorn, 1861.

*New York Daily Tribune*, The, "The Right of Secession," 17 December 1860, in Howard Cecil Perkins, ed., *Northern Editorials on Secession.* Gloucester: Peter Smith, 1964, 199-201.

*New York Evening Post*, "What Shall Be Done for a Revenue?," March 12, 1861, in Howard Cecil Perkins, ed., *Northern Editorials on Secession.* Gloucester: Peter Smith, 1964, Volume II, 599.

*New York Times*, The, March 22-23, 1861, as quoted in Charles Adams, *When in the Course of Human Events, Arguing the Case for Southern Secession.* Lanham: Rowman & Littlefield Publishers, Inc., 2000, 65.

"Ordinance to Repeal the Ratification of the Constitution of the United States of America by the State of Virginia, and to Resume All the Rights and Powers Granted Under said Constitution, Adopted by the Virginia Secession Convention on April 17, 1861," in *The War of the Rebellion: A Compilation of the Official Records of the Union and Confederate Armies.* Washington: Government Printing Office, 1900; reprint, Historical Times, Inc., 1985, Series IV, Volume 1.

Perry, M. S. "Address by Florida Governor M. S. Perry to the Florida Senate and House of Representatives in Tallahassee on 2 February 1861," in *The War of the Rebellion: A Compilation of the Official Records of the Union and Confederate Armies.* Washington: Government Printing Office, 1900; reprint, Historical Times, Inc., 1985, Series IV, Volume 1.

Pickens, Francis Wilkinson. "Inaugural Message of South Carolina Governor Francis Wilkinson Pickens," published 18 December 1860 in *The (Charleston, S.C.) Courier. Quarterly Review, The.*

Potter, David M. *The Impending Crisis, 1848-1861*, completed and edited by Don E. Fehrenbacher. New York: Harper & Row, Publishers, 1976.

Potter, David M. *Lincoln and His Party in the Secession Crisis.* New Haven: Yale University Press, 1942, 1979.

Ramsdell, Charles W. "Lincoln and Fort Sumter," *Journal of Southern History,* Volume 3, Issue 3, August, 1937.

Ramsdell, Charles W. "The Natural Limits of Slavery Expansion," in Edwin C. Rozwenc, ed., *The Causes of the American Civil War.* Boston: D. C. Heath and Company, 1961.

Reagan, John H. "Letter from Hon. John H. Reagan, Member of the United States House of Representatives from Texas, October 19, 1860," in the *Texas (Marshall) Republican,* November 3, 1860.

"Report on the Causes of the Secession of Georgia, adopted by the Georgia Secession Convention, Tuesday, January 29, 1861," in the *Journal of the Georgia Convention, in The War of the Rebellion: A Compilation of the Official Records of the Union and Confederate Armies.* Washington: Government Printing Office, 1900; reprint, Historical Times, Inc., 1985, Series IV, Volume 1.

# Bibliography

"Republican Party Platform, The 1860," in Marshall L. DeRosa, ed., *The Politics of Dissolution, The Quest for a National Identity & the American Civil War*. New Brunswick: Transaction Publishers, 1998.

Roland, Charles P. *An American Iliad, The Story of the Civil War*. Lexington: University Press of Kentucky, 1991.

*Saturday Review*, "The American Tariff Bill," 9 March 1861, 234-235, in Charles Adams, *When in the Course of Human Events, Arguing the Case for Southern Secession*. Lanham: Rowman & Littlefield Publishers, Inc., 2000, 90-91.

"Secessionist Speech, Tuesday Evening, November 13" delivered to the Georgia legislature in Milledgeville, November 13, 1860, in William W. Freehling, and Craig M. Simpson, *Secession Debated, Georgia's Showdown in 1860*. New York: Oxford University Press, 1992.

Seward, William H. "On the Irrepressible Conflict," speech at Rochester, New York, October 25, 1858, in James Buchanan, "Republican Fanatacism as a Cause of the Civil War," in Edwin C. Rozwenc, ed., *The Causes of the American Civil War*. Boston: D. C. Heath and Company, 1961, 61.

Shillingsburg, Miriam J. "Simms's Failed Lecture Tour of 1856: The Mind of the North" in John C. Guilds, ed., *Long Years of Neglect, The Work and Reputation of William Gilmore Simms*. Fayetteville: The University of Arkansas Press, 1988.

Sifakis, Stewart. *Who Was Who in the Civil War*. New York: Facts on File Publications, 1988.

Simkins, Francis Butler & Charles Pierce Roland. *A History of the South,* Forth Edition. New York: Alfred A. Knopf, 1972.

Simms, William Gilmore. "The Antagonisms of the Social Moral. North and South," unpublished 1857 lecture housed in the Charles Carroll Simms

Collection of the South Carolina Library, University of South Carolina, Columbia. "Our Social Moral," also labeled "The Social Moral. Lecture 2," unpublished 1857 lecture housed in the Charles Carroll Simms Collection of the South Carolina Library, University of South Carolina, Columbia. "South Carolina in the Revolution. The Social Moral. Lecture 1", unpublished 1857 lecture housed in the Charles Carroll Simms Collection of the South Carolina Library, University of South Carolina, Columbia.

Smith, Robert H. "An Address to the Citizens of Alabama on the Constitution and Laws of the Confederate States of America. Mobile: 1861.

"Speech of Representative John H. Reagan of Texas, January 15, 1861," in Congressional Globe, 36 Congress, 2 Session, I, 391, abridged, in Kenneth M. Stampp, ed., *The Causes of the Civil War,* 3rd revised edition. New York: Simon & Schuster, Inc., 1991.

Stampp, Kenneth M., ed. *The Causes of the Civil War,* 3rd revised edition. New York: Simon & Schuster, 1959, 1991.

Stampp, Kenneth M. *The Imperiled Union, Essays on the Background of the Civil War.* New York: Oxford University Press, 1980.

Tarbell, Ida M. *The Tariff in Our Times.* New York: The Macmillan Company, 1911.

"The Confederate Struggle" 112 (1862): 537, in Charles Adams, *When in the Course of Human Events, Arguing the Case for Southern Secession.* Lanham: Rowman & Littlefield Publishers, Inc., 2000, 81-82.

"The Rise and Fall of the Confederate Government." New York: D. Appleton and Company, 1912 in William C. Wright, *The Secession Movement in the Middle Atlantic States.* Rutherford: Fairleigh Dickinson University Press, 1973, 14-15.

# Bibliography

Tilley, John Shipley. *Lincoln Takes Command.* Nashville: Bill Coats, Ltd., 1991.

Tocqueville, Alexis de. *Democracy in America,* trans. by George Lawrence. New York: Harper & Row, 1969, Volume 1, 342, in Jeffrey Rogers Hummel *Emancipating Slaves, Enslaving Free Men, A History of the American Civil War.* Chicago: Open Court, 1996, 26.

Toombs, Robert. "On Secession," the last address of Georgia Sen. Robert Toombs in the United States Senate, 7 January 1861, in John Vance Cheney, ed., *Memorable American Speeches, Volume IV, Secession, War, Reconstruction.* Chicago: The Lakeside Press, 1910.

Vanauken, Sheldon. *The Glittering Illusion, English Sympathy for the Southern Confederacy.* Washington: Regnery Gateway, 1989.

Van Deusen, John G. *Economic Bases of Disunion in South Carolina.* New York: Columbia University Press, 1928, 1970.

Walther, Eric H. *The Fire-Eaters.* Baton Rouge: Louisiana State University Press, 1992.

*War of the Rebellion, The: A Compilation of the Official Records of the Union and Confederate Armies.* Washington: Government Printing Office, 1900; reprint, Historical Times, Inc., 1985, Series IV, Volume 1.

Wood, Fernando, N.Y. Mayor, "Mayor Fernando Wood's Recommendation for the Secession of New York City," January 6, 1861, in Henry Steele Commager, ed., *Documents of American History,* Seventh Edition. New York: Appleton- Century-Crofts, 1963.

Wooster, Ralph A. *The Secession Conventions of the South.* Princeton: Princeton University Press, 1962.

Wright, A. R. "Letter of Commissioner A. R. Wright of Georgia to Governor Thomas H. Hicks of Maryland, 25 February 1861," in *The War of the Rebellion: A Compilation of the Official Records of the Union and Confederate*

*Armies*. Washington: Government Printing Office, 1900; reprint, Historical Times, Inc., 1985, Series IV, Volume 1.

Wright, Gavin. *The Political Economy of the Cotton South, Households, Markets, and Wealth in the Nineteenth Century*. New York: W. W. Norton & Company, 1978.

Wright, William C. *The Secession Movement in the Middle Atlantic States*. Rutherford: Fairleigh Dickinson University Press, 1973.

Yanak, Ted, & Pam Cornelison. *The Great American History Fact-Finder*. Boston: Houghton Mifflin Company, 1993.

Yancy, William Lowndes, "Equal Rights in a Common Government, Speech delivered at Washington, D.C., September 21, 1860," in Edwin Anderson Alderman and Joel Chandler Harris, eds., *Library of Southern Literature*. Atlanta: The Martin and Hoyt Company, 1907, Volume 13. Secondary Sources.

Yearns, W. Buck, ed. *The Confederate Governors*. Athens: The University of Georgia Press, 1985. Spring 2011 *Magazine of the Museum of the Confederacy*.

# Index

## A

## B

# Index

175

# Index

3rd, 82
4th, 119
5th, 19, 134
5th Cavalry, 107, 108, 111, 128
6th, 136-37
7th, 84, 119, 153
8th, 19, 134
9th, 134
10th, 134
11th, 117, 134, 139
Florida Atlantic and Gulf Central
    Railroad, 69
Florida Cavalry Battalion, 127
Florida Civil War Centennial
    Commission, 16
Florida General Assembly, 8
*Florida Historical Quarterly*, 105, 115
Florida Hospital, 56
Florida Light Artillery, 65, 90
Florida Railroad, 26, 39
Florida Secession Convention, 34, 133
*Florida Sentinel*, 49
Florida State University, 46, 105
Florida Supreme Court, 8, 13-14, 38
*Florida Union*, 106
Florida, Atlantic, & Gulf Central
    Railroad, 89
*Florida*, CSS, 40, 144
*Floridian*, 106, 113, 115
Floyd, John, B., 50
Ford, John S., 157
Forney, John, 155
Forrest, Nathan Bedford, 155
Fort Barrancas, 21, 23, 61, 64, 102
Fort Brooke, 77, 79-80
Fort Butler, 123
Fort Clinch, 21
Fort Higginson, 69, 70
Fort Jefferson, 21-22
Fort King, 119

Fort Lafayette, 148
Fort Marion, 12, 21
Fort McRee, 23-24, 61, 63-64
Fort Meade, 84-88
Fort Montgomery, 69
Fort Myers, 58, 82-85, 87, 105, 114
Fort Pickens, 21, 23-24, 29, 61-64
Fort Sumter, 5, 15, 62, 63
Fort Taylor, 21
Fox, George B., 130
Franklin, Battle of, 142
Franklin-Nashville Campaign, 119
Free Soil Party, 5
Free Soil Principles. *See* Free Soil
    Party
Free Soilers. *See* Free Soil Principles
Freedman's Aid Society, 59
Fugitive Slave Act, 5

# G

Gadsden County (FL), 111
Gadsden Grays, 108, 111
Gainesville (FL), 85, 95-100, 122, 127-
    28, 130-32, 138
Galveston (TX), 145
Gamble Mansion, 55
Gamble, Robert H., 90, 91
Gamble's Light Artillery, 92
Gammon, William Lamar, 34
Garden Key (FL), 21
*General Edmund Kirby Smith, C.S.A.*,
    158
General Tax Act (1863), 38
Georgetown College. *See* Georgetown
    University
Georgetown University, 140
Georgia, 9, 11-13, 41, 46, 51, 67, 73, 89,
    102, 106, 109, 132, 142, 151, 153
    1st, 90-92
    4th Cavalry, 90

177

# Index

# M

# Index

# Index

## S

Saint Andrews Bay (FL), 40
Salvor, 77
San Francisco (CA), 145
Sanborn, Frank, 125, 126
Sanderson (FL), 89, 93
Sanderson Station (FL), 95
Sanderson, John P., 16
Santa Ana, Antonio Lopez, 139
Santa Rosa Island (FL), 21, 23, 61, 63
Santo Domingo, 8, 12
Sarasota Bayou (FL), 57
Saunders (FL), 124
Savannah (GA), 50, 72, 74, 134
Savannah, Albany, & Georgia
    Railroad, 106
Sayler's Creek, Battle of, 118
Scotland, 58
Scott, Winfield, 154
*Scottish Chief*, The, 78-80
Second Manassas, Battle of, 32
Second Military District Department
    of Mississippi and East Louisiana
    (CSA), 141
Second Seminole War, 139, 150
Seminole. *See* Smith, Edmund Kirby
Seminole Indians, 119, 139
Seminole War, 85, 87, 136
Semmes, Alex, 80
Semmes, Raphael, 145
*Sentinel* (Tallahassee), 10
Settleworth, W.P., 96
Seven Days, Battle of, 32
Sewanee, Tennessee, 157
Seward, Henry, 3, 61, 165
Seymour, Truman, 72, 74, 89, 91, 93-95
*Shenandoah*, CSS, 145-46, 149
Sherman, Thomas W., 67
Sherman, William T., 84, 114

Shiloh, Battle of, 32
Simmons, Henry K., 109, 111
Slemmer, Adam J., 61
Smith, Caraway, 90, 109, 110
Smith, Edmund Kirby, 18, 136, 154-58
Smith, Ephraim Kirby, 154, 158
Smith, Joseph Lee, 154
Smyrna (FL), 132
South Atlantic Squadron, 29
South Carolina, 9, 11, 46, 73, 121, 132
    1st (USCT), 68
    2nd (USCT), 68
    11th, 75
South Florida, 46, 59, 84, 100
South Florida Bulldogs. *See* 7th
    Florida Infantry Regiment
Spain, 14
Spencer, W.B., 126
Spratt, L.W., 11
*Spray*, The, 108
St. Andrews Bay (FL), 44, 103
St. Augustine (FL), 7, 9, 12, 21, 27, 29,
    53, 58, 114, 122, 139-40, 151, 154
St. George Rogers, S., 16
St. Johns Bar, 65
St. Johns Bluff (FL), 29, 31, 65-66, 68,
    135
St. John's Church, 70
St. Johns River, 19-20, 29, 31, 54, 65-
    66, 68, 71, 74, 93, 98, 122-23, 127,
    130, 132
St. Luke's Episcopal Church
    (Tallahasee), 118, 152
St. Luke's Episcopal Church
    (Marianna), 103
St. Marks (FL), 18, 20, 25, 106-08
St. Marks River, 105, 107
St. Marys (FL), 27
Starke (FL), 98, 127, 129
Starke, Mary, 153

# Index

www.ingramcontent.com/pod-product-compliance
Lightning Source LLC
Chambersburg PA
CBHW031840090426
42741CB00005B/302